VISIBILITY
5

Success Stories from Leaders Making
an Impact from the Stage

DANNELLA BURNETT

HybridGlobal
PUBLISHING

Published by
Hybrid Global Publishing
333 E 14th Street
#3C
New York, NY 10003

Manufactured in the United States of America, or in the United Kingdom when distributed elsewhere.

Burnett, Dannella
Visibility 5: Success Stories from Leaders Making an Impact from the Stage

Paperback ISBN: 978-1-938015-13-7 (paperback)
ISBN: 978-1-938015-14-4 (eBook)

Cover design: Joe Potter
Book Interior and eBook design by: Amit Dey
Copyediting: Claudia Volkman

Website: https://dannella360.com/

Disclaimer
The information provided in this book is intended for entertainment and general informational purposes. Some stories reference real individuals and companies, while others have been adapted, fictionalized or amalgamated to illustrate broader principles and ideas. Readers are advised to consult with a licensed professional before making any investment decisions. The author and publisher assume no liability for financial outcomes resulting from actions based on the content of this book.

CONTENTS

CONTENTS

FOREWORD

It's time for you to be visible—"in the spotlight"!

We all have a story, a message, and a desire to make a difference during our lifetime and careers. That's why I am so excited to promote this wonderful book *Visibility*, by global transformational leader and marketing expert Dannella Burnett, who has spent her career helping people to be visible and make an impact in their lives and career.

You will hear stories and strategies from incredible entrepreneurs and influencers making an impact against all odds, and one strategy in this book could make ALL the difference in your journey to the influence you desire.

My visibility story starts when I was very young. When I was a teenager, NBC put me under contract with a starring role in their television sitcom *Gimme a Break*. Appearing weekly on NBC, along with *Family Ties*, *Facts of Life*, and *Hill Street Blues* made me very visible very fast! Starring in a network television series was something I'd always dreamed of achieving as a young child, and when it happened, I was thrilled. But quite honestly, I was a little unprepared for how visible I would become—all over the world . . . overnight!

I had to learn *very* quickly how to handle the media spotlight. One of my responsibilities was go on a press tour. I appeared as a guest on many classic shows like *The Today Show*, *Merv Griffin*, and of course *Entertainment Tonight*. Promoting our series was a new technique—one I didn't have any expertise in. I was an actor, not a public relations expert. But there were some amazing executives in the NBC publicity department who taught me about public relations and how to promote. I am also very grateful to my Beverly Hills publicist who mentored me and gave me wonderful notes every time I appeared in the media.

So how can my experience help you to become more visible?

I have learned that you can have the best message, product, or service in the world, but if you don't know how to promote it, it won't be successful.

Over the years, I have seen so many talented actors and entrepreneurs who never reached their potential because they didn't have the RIGHT promotional strategy, and they didn't know how to promote themselves effectively.

I also recognized that my credibility from being visible for so many decades opened doors for me that never would have opened without it.

This is why the techniques of being visible and promoting yourself effectively are essential to achieving success.

In this book, you will hear stories and strategies from many people who had big dreams, have achieved their goals, and are continuing to build their visibility and impact.

Being visible and promoting yourself is a delicate process. You don't want to come off egotistical or self-involved, and there are simple yet very specific strategies and techniques to do promote yourself effectively.

One of the most important things I have learned is the power of having other people promote you and speak highly of you. Third-party credibility is very powerful when you are introduced as a guest in the media. Television and print media, being a guest on a popular podcast, and speaking on stages are all ways that can give you the credibility you have been lacking in the past.

People need to respect you before they will receive your message, and that literally can be achieved in less than ninety seconds! And then, of course, you need to build trust.

I currently produce and host a television show on ABC called *In the Spotlight* featuring celebrities, business owners, beautiful travel destinations, and nonprofit organizations. One of the most important things we do when working with a guest (who is a not celebrity) is teach them how to tell their story and why they are so passionate about what they do in one minute or less. Learning this technique and how to be effective when sharing your passion and your product or service will transform your success for lifelong impact.

My most helpful tip: If you don't have a promotional video on the top of the fold of your website and pinned to the top of your social media that explains who you are and how you've helped people, this must be at the TOP of your to-do list.

A ninety-second branding video can make you visible, respected, and understood before you ever say a word. Hollywood uses this technique every Day with their commercials and trailers.

I've been blessed to watch many of my clients and guests have a complete turnaround in their business financially by learning how to promote themselves effectively on television, on stage, and online. Learning how to effectively speak in sound bites has completely transformed their businesses!

Will this be a new skill you haven't tried before? Yes! And will it be a little uncomfortable at first? Yes! But the rewards will be immeasurable!

Picture anyone you respect. When you see them in the media or on social media, are they powerful at sharing their message and being visible? Of course they are. They have mastered the art of visibility and Promotion. And the great news is that this is a skill you can learn. It may not happen overnight, but don't ever give up on your dream—it was put in your heart for a reason, and you can achieve it if you just don't give up! Surround yourself with people who can teach you how to be more visible and promote yourself effectively.

The pages of this book can be an inspiration and a guide for those of you who have struggled with visibility in the past.

Thank you, Dannella, for asking me to share my experience of visibility, and for your unwavering support of those who are determined to make a difference during their lives and to have a voice that is finally heard.

The only way to make that happen is to be visible, and I applaud you, Dannella, for your series of *Visibility* books that give so many talented people an opportunity to pay it forward with their inspiring stories!

I am very excited for all of you who are about to take this journey, because I know it's time for you to be in the spotlight!

With love and excitement for your visibility journey,

Kari Michaelsen

Kari Michaelsen is a highly sought-after public speaker and trainer. As a teen, she starred in the NBC hit TV series *Gimme a Break*. She has interviewed and shared the stage with many of the greatest leaders and achievers of our time. Today she is the producer and host of *In the Spotlight* on ABC, where she features celebrities, entrepreneurs, and nonprofit organizations.

inthespotlight.tv

THE VISIBILITY PARADOX: WHY BEING SEEN MATTERS MORE THAN BEING PERFECT

DANNELLA BURNETT

Here's something I've learned after decades of producing events, working with speakers, and building my own business: You can have the best idea, the most powerful story, and the most life-changing offer— but if no one knows who you are, it doesn't matter.

That's where visibility comes in.

But let's be real. Visibility is tricky. On one hand, it's the thing we know we need most as entrepreneurs and business owners. On the other hand, it's the thing we resist the hardest. We tell ourselves, "I'll go live when my hair looks better," or "I'll pitch that event once my talk is perfect." Or the big one: "I'll be ready . . . later."

Here's the truth: The stage isn't just where you show your success, it's where you *build* it.

From Behind the Curtain to the Spotlight

For years, I was perfectly content being the one behind the scenes. My background is in events. I loved being the person who made everything seamless while other people got the spotlight. I thought my gift was producing, not speaking.

Honestly, hiding felt safer. I didn't have to worry about whether people liked my story, my outfit, or my delivery. I could just work hard and let other people shine.

But over time, I realized that my staying invisible had a cost. Not just to me, but to the people I was meant to serve. By playing small, I was holding back strategies, lessons, and encouragement that others truly needed.

The first time I stepped out on stage in my own right, I was terrified. My voice shook. My mind went blank more than once. I compared myself to everyone else in the room. But something amazing happened: People leaned in. They didn't care about "perfect." They cared about connection.

That moment taught me that showing up as my real, messy, authentic self was far more powerful than hiding behind a polished façade.

Why Visibility Feels Scary (and Why That's Okay)

Let's be honest. Being visible feels scary because it *is* scary. You're opening yourself up to judgment, to criticism, to the possibility of getting it wrong.

But flip it around. You're also opening yourself up to opportunities, to connections, to impact.

Fear and growth often travel together. So if you're nervous about putting yourself out there, take that as a good sign. It means you're stepping into new territory.

I've worked with so many speakers who tell me they don't want to "bother people," or they're afraid to be too loud, or they worry they'll be judged. And my response is always the same: You already are being judged. People are forming opinions whether you show up or not. So why not at least show up on purpose? And we know we missed 100 percent of the shots we never take. Up your odds by taking action!

The people who avoid visibility might stay comfortable, but they rarely make the kind of impact they're capable of. Playing small has never built a legacy.

The Real Equation

Here's how it actually works:

Visibility → Connection → Opportunity → Impact → Income

Show up, and people connect with you. From those connections come opportunities. Those opportunities create impact. And from impact comes income.

Most people try to reverse it. They chase the income first, then wonder why it doesn't work. It doesn't work because they skipped step one: being visible.

Real Stories of Visibility in Action

I've seen this transformation happen over and over again.

- A brand-new entrepreneur shared her story of loss and resilience at a small local event. She was shaking the whole time. Afterward, she walked away with three collaborations and her first podcast interview. That one moment changed everything for her.

- A coach who swore she would "never do video" finally went live on social media. Within a month, she had an invitation to speak at an international summit. Within a year, her revenue tripled.
- A corporate leader who felt invisible in meetings decided to start a small mastermind group. Suddenly, he wasn't over-looked anymore. He was seen as a thought leader.

Every time, the shift didn't come from being more polished or more qualified. It came from being more visible.

And let me add this: Sometimes visibility looks smaller than a big stage. Sometimes it's introducing yourself at a networking event. Sometimes it's writing that first post on LinkedIn. Sometimes it's asking a question from the audience instead of staying quiet. Visibility is built in those everyday choices.

A Behind-the-Scenes Realization

An event I produced years ago drove this home for me. I was backstage, making sure everything was running smoothly, when I watched a speaker step out for the very first time. She was visibly shaking. Her notes were crumpled in her hand.

She shared her story with so much honesty that the whole room leaned in. People cried. People laughed. At the end, she got a standing ovation, and I saw her collecting money for her book sales and making appointments to follow up. I saw her business taking shape.

In that moment, I realized something. I had been hiding behind the curtain while asking others to step into the spotlight. If she could be brave enough to show up messy and real, what excuse did I have to keep hiding? That realization changed everything for me.

It allowed my business to grow to seven figures in eighteen months and stay there through speaking and events.

The Visibility Paradox

Here's what I call the Visibility Paradox:

- You think you need confidence before you show up. The truth: Confidence comes *after* you show up.
- You think you need clarity before you speak out. The truth: Clarity comes *because* you speak out.
- You think you need a perfect plan. The truth: You just need to start.

We keep waiting for the right time, but "ready" is an illusion. The stage is what makes you ready.

Think about it like this. Nobody learns to swim by reading about swimming. You learn by getting in the water, flailing a little, sputtering a little, and then figuring it out. Visibility works the same way.

Visibility Is Leadership

Let this really sink in: Visibility isn't just marketing. It's leadership.

When you show up, you give others permission to do the same. You model courage. You become a possibility for someone else.

Think about the leaders who inspire you most. It isn't their perfection that makes them unforgettable. It's their willingness to be real, to share the messy parts, to be human.

If you want to create impact, if you want to leave a legacy, you can't do it hiding in the shadows.

Simple Ways to Start Being More Visible

You don't have to start with a giant stage or a TEDx Talk. Start small and build momentum.

1. Own your story. The messy parts are the gold. Stop editing them out.
2. Start small. Go live for five minutes, say yes to a panel, record a podcast interview.
3. Be consistent. Visibility is built through repetition. Show up weekly, not once in a while.
4. Find your people. Surround yourself with a community that cheers you on and reminds you why you matter.
5. Have an offer. Visibility is wonderful, but pair it with a way people can take the next step with you. That's where visibility turns into income.

And here's a bonus tip: Celebrate the small wins. Don't wait until you land the "big stage" to pat yourself on the back. Every step into visibility counts.

Myths about Visibility

Let's bust a few myths I hear all the time:

- Myth: I need to have a huge following first.

  No, you don't. Start with the people right in front of you. A room of ten people can change your business if you show up fully.

- Myth: I need to be polished and perfect.

  No again. People don't connect with perfect. They connect with real.

- Myth: Visibility is for extroverts.

  Absolutely not. Some of the most powerful speakers I know are introverts. They just learned how to use their voice in a way that fits them.

At the Heart of It

Visibility is not about ego. It's about service.

When you show up, someone who feels stuck sees hope. Someone who is searching finds answers. Someone who feels alone realizes they are not.

For me, it is also about legacy. My children are stepping into adulthood now, and I want them to see what it looks like to live boldly. To take up space. To use your gifts without apology. That is what visibility means to me.

Your Stage Is Waiting

Here's the truth. Opportunities are everywhere. Stages are everywhere. What is rare is the person willing to say yes to being visible.

You don't need to wait for permission. You don't need to wait for perfection. You don't need to wait for the "right" time.

You just need to start.

Because visibility isn't the prize you get once you've succeeded. It's the path that gets you there.

And the world is waiting to see you.

Dannella Burnett is a speaker, event producer, and visibility strategist who helps entrepreneurs, coaches, and leaders get booked, get seen, and get paid from every stage. As founder of Encore Elite Events and Speakers Need to Speak, she has produced thousands of events and guided hundreds of experts to amplify their message, monetize their influence, and leave a legacy of impact through speaking and events.

encoreeliteevents.com

FROM SILENCE TO DEEP CONNECTION: FINDING THE COURAGE TO SHARE YOUR DEEPEST DESIRES

Mark Allen

Have you ever lay awake at 3:00 a.m., staring at the ceiling, your mind racing with a desire so intense it feels like it might burst out of your chest?

You know the one I'm talking about.

That thing you want so desperately you can practically taste it.

But every time you think about bringing it up with your partner, your throat goes desert-dry.

I'll bet you have!

We all do.

It's that invisible wall we build around our most vulnerable desires, convinced that speaking them out loud might shatter everything we've worked so hard to create.

But here's the thing: What if that silence is slowly suffocating the very relationship you're trying to protect?

Let's face it—most of us would rather endure the slow burn of unexpressed desire than risk the potential explosion of honest conversation. It's like we're all walking around with loaded emotional guns, too scared to even acknowledge they exist.

I remember when this reality hit home for me. It was during my awkward high school years. I was the quintessential shy, nerdy kid who couldn't even muster up the courage to talk to girls, let alone ask them out. I couldn't express what I actually wanted from anyone. It felt like I was suffocating in my own silence.

Then came college and my first (and only) blind date. Picture me: a bundle of nerves, my knees shaking so hard I thought they might register on the Richter scale. I half expected to vibrate right off my chair! But when she walked in, something magical happened. For the first time in my life, words came easily. And now, nearly forty years later, we're still together.

Our wedding in Hawaii was like a scene from a movie: palm trees, ocean breezes, feet in the sand. Perfect, right? Well, almost. I had this nagging feeling, a part of me I'd never shown her. A desire I'd buried so deep I could barely admit it to myself.

As the years went by, Beth and I found ourselves drifting apart. We weren't fighting, but we both knew something was missing. That spark, the excitement we once had, seemed to have dimmed. We were going through the motions, like two actors who'd forgotten we were supposed to be playing lovers instead of roommates.

Meanwhile, this desire—this thing I wanted so badly I'd wake up at 3:00 a.m. thinking about it—was eating me alive from the inside.

It's that feeling of wanting something so intensely it becomes like a low-grade fever you can't shake. Every conversation with your partner becomes a missed opportunity. Every intimate moment carries the weight of unspoken words.

Now, I'll be honest, my first attempt at broaching the subject with Beth was . . . less than graceful. Let's just say that blurting out your deepest desire while driving isn't exactly the most romantic approach. It caught her completely off guard and could have easily derailed our entire relationship.

Short answer: It didn't.

It also didn't get me what I desired (not immediately). Truthfully, I knew it would take time and lots of honest discussions to make such a change. But sharing it with her was one of the best things I've ever done because it was no longer this big thing between us. The wall had fallen, and we could start to see each other in a new light.

We worked on ourselves individually; we saw counselors and coaches. I even attended a men's retreat to figure out why I was so terrified of my own desires. Beth started exploring what she really wanted too. It was like we were both archaeologists, carefully excavating parts of ourselves we'd buried under years of "supposed tos" and "shoulds."

As we grew closer again, I found the courage to bring up the topic once more. This time, it was during a casual conversation on the couch, my head in her lap, when I suggested finding a group of couples to go dancing with. Beth saw right through me and asked if I still wanted to explore swinging. I looked her in the eyes and said, "Yes, I really do!"

To my surprise, she actually was open to it. We had done so much work on ourselves and our relationship that there was enough trust to consider exploring new ways of connecting. We had built a strong foundation for our relationship, and now we felt secure enough to move forward.

That conversation in the car years earlier had changed everything. For the first time in our marriage, I had been completely, vulnerably honest about who I was and what I desired.

And you know what happened? The world didn't end. Our marriage didn't implode. Instead, something beautiful began to unfold.

We started having conversations we'd never had before. Real conversations about desire, fear, dreams, and the parts of ourselves we'd kept hidden. There was a newfound freedom in our relationship. Standing there, emotionally naked, we realized there was nothing left to hide.

This journey brought a renewed sense of intimacy to both of us. We got to rediscover each other as whole, complex human beings with depths we'd never fully explored. It's like finding secret rooms in a house you thought you knew every corner of.

Now, I help other couples navigate this terrifying, beautiful journey of authentic communication. I guide them in finding the courage to share their deepest desires in a way that honors their relationship. We work on dismantling the fear that honest desire will destroy love.

Here's what I've learned: There are as many desires as there are people on this planet. Your desire isn't wrong, weird, or dangerous simply because you've been afraid to voice it.

Through this journey, we've discovered that authentic intimacy isn't possible without authentic expression. When we navigate our deepest conversations with respect, trust, and powerful communication, we're not just helping our relationships survive—we're helping them come alive.

But let me be clear: This journey isn't always smooth sailing. There are moments of terror, times when you'll want to take back every word you've said, and yes, sometimes the response isn't what you hoped for. But here's the beautiful truth—even a "no" delivered with love and understanding is infinitely better than a lifetime of wondering "what if."

I remember the morning after I finally shared my deepest desire with Beth. I woke up expecting to feel exposed and vulnerable. Instead, I felt . . . lighter. Like I'd been carrying a boulder on my back for years and had finally set it down. Even though we were still figuring out what my honesty meant for us, the relief of being truly known was overwhelming.

That's the magic of courageous honesty. It's not about getting what you want—it's about being seen and loved for who you really are, desires and all.

One of the most beautiful things I've witnessed in this work is how sharing one buried desire often opens the floodgates for both partners. I've seen couples discover they've been hiding complementary longings. I've watched relationships transform from polite coexistence to passionate partnership.

And it's not just about the big, scary desires. It's about creating a relationship where you can share the small wants too—the everyday longings that make up the texture of a life lived authentically together.

When you can talk openly about what you really want, when you can support your partner's growth and exploration, it creates a level of trust that's truly profound. It's like moving from a black-and-white movie to full color.

So, if you're lying awake at night with that desire burning in your chest, know that you're not alone. There's no wrong way to want. Your longing is valid. Your courage to share it is a gift to your relationship.

Who knows? You might just find a deeper, more fulfilling connection than you ever thought possible.

Love grows when we feed it truth. The more we open our hearts to honest expression, the more love we have to give and receive. Just like a garden—the more you tend to it with authentic care, the more it flourishes.

Sharing your deepest desires isn't a magic fix for relationship problems. It won't solve every issue or miraculously transform a struggling partnership overnight. In fact, it might shine a spotlight on areas that need work. But for couples who are willing to walk through the fear together, it can open up a world of intimacy they never knew was possible.

It's about creating a relationship that truly reflects who you are and what you want rather than who you think you should be. It's about writing your own story of love—one that honors your deepest truths, not those of others or society.

So, embrace the fear, lean into the conversation, and let authentic desire transform your connection into something extraordinary.

Because on the other side of that terrifying conversation? That's where real love lives.

As a pioneering relationship coach, **Mark Allen** leverages his experience from thirty-three years of marriage to help couples unlock their hidden desires and share them with each other. Through practical communication strategies and transformational insights, Mark guides couples to break free from conventional limits and embrace honest dialogue that leads to profound connection, trust, and mutual fulfillment.

openingus.com

VISIBILITY ISN'T JUST ABOUT BEING SEEN—IT'S ABOUT BEING WILLING

SHIRAZ BABOO

L et's talk visibility.

Everyone and their dog is shouting about the need to "be seen," "go viral," or "show up consistently." And while they're not wrong, they're also not telling you what's *actually* going on underneath that surface-level advice.

Because visibility—real, impactful, soul-level visibility—isn't a marketing strategy.

It's an identity shift.

And if you're stuck, spinning, second-guessing, or self-sabotaging, it's not because your content strategy sucks. It's because you're running an unconscious story that says: Being visible is not safe.

And your brain? It's really good at keeping you safe. Even if it means keeping you invisible and possibly broke.

You're Not Addicted to Struggle; You're Addicted to the Chemical High of Being Invisible

Sounds a bit crazy? Let me explain.

We've all got stories. Some are empowering, like "I always find the best parking spots." (Mine is "Things are always working out for me.")

Others are not so helpful. For instance, "If I show up and be visible, people won't like me," or "I might feel humiliated if I say the wrong thing on stage."

But here's where your mind gets really sneaky. Once a story has been running for long enough, you don't just *believe* it—you become *chemically addicted* to the emotions that story generates.

Every time you "stay safe" by not posting, not launching, not speaking up? You get a hit of dopamine. Maybe some serotonin. And possibly even adrenaline.

It's a drug cocktail your body craves. It feels great in the moment even though there are emotions such as frustration, fear, anxiety, or guilt before and after. As long as your body gets its fix, its happy.

I call this **reality addiction**: You're addicted to the *proof* that your stories are true. Even when they suck.

You Can't Be Seen When You're Covered in Snow

Here's a visual for you.

Imagine you're a beautiful car. Sexy, sleek, powerful.

Now, imagine that before you've even pulled out of the driveway, you're covered in snow. Heavy snow. Decades of snow. This snow is made up of the limiting beliefs you've picked up in life. Not just from your family, but your culture, your school, your religion, the media, your ex, your first grade teacher, and that one networking group you thought was a good idea but made you feel like garbage. You get the idea.

All the beliefs that tell you:

- "Don't rock the boat."

- "It's selfish to shine."
- "Put yourself last."
- "Be safe."
- "Don't make too much money."
- "Don't stand out."

So now you're trying to drive through the world with all this on top of you. You're trying to create impact and income while buried under five feet of snow and looking through a small section of window you managed to clear off. Some people never even get off the driveway. That is, they don't even attempt to go after their dreams.

Here's the kicker. You can just shovel it off. It's just that no one taught you that.

Yet you absolutely can.

The Visibility Trap: Blocks, Not Just Strategy Gaps

I see it all the time. People trying to use brute force to push through the blocks.

Let's say you're trying to build your business.

You've got your funnel set up. You've done the branding shoot. You're batching reels like a maniac. And still . . . crickets.

Here's the thing: You're not lazy. You're not untalented. You are blocked.

Blocks are things your subconscious creates to stop you from getting the thing you say you want. Because getting that thing would trigger an even bigger fear.

Like:

- "If I get more visible, I'll be judged."
- "If I become successful, my friends/family will reject me."
- "If I stand out, I'll get canceled or attacked."

So your brain thinks, "Yeah, we're not doing that."

You'll ghost your own launch. Or make your tech break. Or "coincidentally" get sick the day before a big speaking gig.

And then, to soothe the sting, your body hits you with a chemical fix.

- "I knew it wouldn't work."
- "There it goes again."
- "Every time I almost succeed, something happens."

You get to be right. You get your dopamine hit. You stay stuck. And you feel safe. It sucks, but it's safe because you know the story. You know the outcome. There are no unknowns that await in the world of being visible and successful. Whew.

Visibility Without Guilt

Let's be honest, visibility can make people feel guilty.

Guilt for shining too much.
Guilt for not being "humble" enough.
Guilt for out-earning your parents, your friends, your clients.

And your family, your community, your friends all have stories about rich people being greedy, fame being dangerous, or visibility being ego, so that even wanting visibility can feel like betrayal.

I once worked with a client who couldn't grow her business past a certain point, not because of her skill, but because every time she edged toward "rich," she unconsciously heard her family motto: "You can be rich and miserable, or you can be poor and happy." So her subconscious decided, "I want to be happy, so I'll be poor."

But guess what? She wasn't happy. She was frustrated. She was angry. And her mind comforted her by saying, "At least you're not miserable." Of course, it didn't even occur to her that the story was false—that it's what her parents said to justify their income.

She didn't need a better business coach. She needed a new story. When we removed that story, she immediately started making money.

You Don't Have to Prove Yourself to Be Seen

A lot of people are taught that in order to be seen, you have to prove yourself.

You need to show how hard you've worked, how much you've sacrificed, how much you've suffered. I call this the "martyr visibility" model.

It sounds like:

- "I barely slept but I crushed it."
- "I worked 12 hours straight on this launch."
- "This took *everything* out of me, but it was worth it."

You say it to yourself and others. And when you say it to others, they give you your fix through love.

- "Wow, you're a machine! I'm impressed."
- "Hang in there. It'll pay off."
- "You really deserve a lot after all that hard work!"

Guess what you get besides dopamine? Oxytocin! The love chemical. Your body loves that. (Pun intended.)

So now your story is that you must earn visibility through pain to get love, and pain becomes your strategy.

It's exhausting and unnecessary.

You don't need to show the blood, sweat, and tears. You just need to show *you*.

So . . . How Do You Get Unblocked?

Great question. I'm glad you asked. Let's keep it simple:

1. Notice the story.

Start with curiosity, not condemnation.

Ask yourself, "What is the hidden benefit I'm getting by staying in this story?" It's always going to be about avoiding a negative emotion or getting a positive one, like the love fix above.

Don't try to fix it. Just notice it.

Because once you see it, it's no longer running the show unconsciously.

2. Decide if the story is still serving you.

Not every story is bad, so ask, "Does this story get me closer to the life I want, or keep me in the life I have?"

3. Step Out of the Story.

If your story isn't serving you, it's time to let it go. Decide you're done with it—you're stepping out of that story. And if there's a better story, step in to that one instead.

For instance, I used to work hard all the time. When I realized I was burning myself out, I decided to create a story that things happen easily for me. As I anchored in each time something happened easily for me, the amount of things that were hard started to decrease. Now, for the most part, everything is easy.

It's easier to replace one addiction with another than just remove the bad addiction, so do this wherever you can.

Visibility as a Spiritual Practice

Real visibility—the kind that leads to impact, income, and joy—requires you to be radically honest with yourself.

It's not about being louder. It's about being clearer.

It's not about being perfect. It's about being real.
It's about rewriting the stories that say:

- "You don't deserve attention."
- "You're not ready yet."
- "Visibility is unsafe."

And replacing them with ones that say:

- "Your voice matters."
- "Your story helps others."
- "You were born to be seen."

You don't need to go viral.

You need to go visible: energetically, emotionally, and unapologetically.

Final Truth Bomb: Visibility Won't Kill You—But Staying Hidden Might

Not physically. But spiritually? Creatively? Financially?

Yes.

Because when you stay hidden, you stay disconnected from your purpose. You create a loop of frustration where you're doing all the things and getting none of the results. And you wonder what's wrong with you.

There's nothing wrong with you. There's just a story running your life, and a chemical addiction feeding that story.

But once you're willing to see the story, question it, and choose a new one, you become the author of your life again.

And that's when the world starts to see you.

Shiraz Baboo is a multi-award-winning author, international speaker, and Reality Interventionist™ who helps people rewrite the unconscious stories keeping them stuck. Known for his work on *Reality Addiction™*, he empowers entrepreneurs to shift out of struggle and into success. His book *How to Rewrite Reality* has transformed lives around the world.

energeticmagic.com

RECLAIM YOUR VOICE

TERI BACH

For most of my childhood, I lived with one quiet fear: that I could be sent back.

I never told anyone that.

I was adopted as a baby, and even though my parents were wonderful and I knew they loved me, my little mind believed there was an invisible return policy. After all, my birth parents hadn't kept me . . .

So, I made a decision to *be the perfect child.*

Never upset anyone.

Never make waves.

Don't argue. Don't cause trouble.

Don't speak up unless you're sure it's safe.

When I was a young child, my mom and I would visit friends. People would ask me questions, and my mom would answer for me. As time went on, this became our pattern; people would ask me a question, and I'd just smile and wait for her to answer for me.

I thought I was being polite.

What I was really doing was disappearing.

I learned to fly under the radar so well you could almost forget I was there. And in the process, I lost my voice.

I was full of ideas, opinions, hopes, and dreams. I was just too scared to say them out loud. Instead of helping me, in reality this was setting me up for unnecessary struggles.

I allowed others to define my identity—who I was, the paths I would take, even my own worth.

Many of us lose our voices during life's transitions: through divorce, empty nests, loss of loved ones, retirement, career changes, because somewhere along the way, we've been taught to play small.

We avoid conflict. We hide our opinions. We stay quiet, thinking it's safer. But here's the truth . . . silence doesn't protect you; it erases you.

Reclaiming your voice is the first step to stepping into the next, better chapter of your life.

But here's the truth: silence may feel safe, but it actually blocks growth. When you suppress your voice, you also suppress your ability to adapt, to create, and to thrive during change.

And when life transitions hit, the only constant you carry forward is your voice.

Your perspective.

Your truth.

Your values.

Years ago, I was married and raising my two-year-old daughter, Sarah. Long story short, I was in the process of a divorce when Sarah tragically passed away. Within two months, I went from being a wife and mother to losing both of those roles.

As you can imagine, it was an incredibly difficult time. The loss of my beautiful Sarah tore my heart out.

Looking back and reflecting on the pain I felt during this time, I see that I had an advantage over others who have gone through similar experiences.

By that time, I had a strong sense of identity. I did not let my previous roles define my worth. I knew exactly who I aspired to be.

I had been very determined to have a career as a psychotherapist. I had dreamed of it for years; before my marriage, before motherhood.

I had one more class to take to get my degree, and I did it. I kept going. I couldn't let my loss impede my future gains.

In your own life, start by asking yourself these different questions:

- *What do I actually believe? What limiting beliefs are holding me back?*
- *What am I no longer willing to settle for?*
- *What excites me enough to get out of bed in the morning?*

Because here's what research tells us:

- **Unhappiness has a financial cost.** Staying silent in the wrong role or relationship can keep you stuck in cycles of lost income, missed promotions, or even financial dependence.
- **Unhappiness damages relationships.** Without your voice, true connection disappears.
- **Unhappiness impacts mental and physical health.** Research shows that long-term dissatisfaction is linked to higher levels of stress, anxiety, depression, and even a weakened immune system. In other words, silence doesn't just steal your joy, it can steal your health.

So, reclaiming your voice isn't just a feel-good idea; it's survival.

It's the difference between living stuck in quiet discontent and stepping forward into the life you were meant to create. If I could go back and talk to my younger self, the first thing I would do is encourage her to speak up.

Tell your story, voice your concerns, take risks. Don't be invisible.

Here's the reality: major life transitions don't just strip away roles, they also strip away the masks we've been wearing.

All those *"should haves"* we carried—how we should look, how we should act, the career we should have had, the life we should be living—suddenly come rushing in.

And if you're not careful, those "shoulds" can become a prison.

They keep you invisible, quietly existing instead of fully living.

Rediscovering who you are is powerful because visibility changes everything.

- **When you're visible, you get your spark back.** After age fifty, so much can shift: kids may be grown, retirement may be on the horizon, and even our brains evolve, giving us a greater sense of independence and perspective. Instead of loss, this time can be the doorway to freedom.

- **Visibility lets you choose, not settle.** This is the moment to ask:
  - What do I want to keep?
  - What do I want to remove?
  - Where do I want to go next?

- **Remaining "content" comes at a cost.** Studies show that long-term complacency accelerates aging, increases depression, and even impacts physical health. When we stay invisible, we shrink. We get older faster. Our bodies show it. Our minds show it. Our joy disappears.

- **Visibility creates wealth inside and out.** When you shine, you also start to uncover hidden patterns in how you see money, worth, and possibility. You tap into new opportunities because you're no longer playing small.

This stage of life after fifty should be the most exciting chapter yet, not a slow fade into the background.

Rediscovering who you are means stepping back into the spotlight, on your terms, with a clarity and confidence you may not have had in your twenties or thirties.

So, let me ask you: If all the "shoulds" were stripped away, and you permitted yourself to be fully visible, who would you become?

If you could build the life you really want without any obstacles, without worrying what others would think, what would it look like? How would your day-to-day be different? Describe your health, overall wellness, and even your finances.

I can tell you right now that the young girl sitting in the kitchen with her mother and friends, terrified to speak up, would be proud of the fearless woman she is today.

Even though it took me a while to discover my identity, once I did, those life transitions didn't become a tragic end; they opened doors to new possibilities.

Here's the truth: No one ever grew inside their comfort zone. If you want something different, you have to take action.

And here's the science: Your brain is designed to protect you, so it labels anything unfamiliar as "danger."

But growth requires retraining your brain to see new experiences not as threats, but as opportunities.

The more often you do this, the easier it becomes to step into change.

I remember a time right after my mom passed away. I felt lost, unsure of what was next. Then an opportunity came up for a trip to Rome, Italy, with nine other women.

Everything in me hesitated. I didn't have a current passport. I didn't know a single person who was going. My inner voice whispered all the reasons to stay home. But I said yes.

There were challenges ... language barriers, getting lost, even the fear of traveling alone. But on the other side of fear came freedom.

I discovered a braver version of myself, one my mom would have been so proud of.

That trip wasn't about Italy. It was about proving to myself that I could do hard things, that I could build a life bigger than my fear.

And here's the secret: We're not meant to do it alone.

Growth sticks when you surround yourself with others who push you, encourage you, and remind you of what's possible.

Whether it's traveling to a new country, starting a business, or speaking up for the first time in years, doing what scares you is powerful, but doing it with others makes it sustainable.

So, here's my challenge to you: Stop waiting for the "right time."

The right time is now.

Take the risk.

Speak up.

Book the trip.

Sign up for the class.

Join the community.

Do the thing that makes your palms sweat.

Because that's the doorway to the life you're dreaming about.

What's one thing that scares you, but excites you enough to change your life? And who can you invite to walk with you through it?

Teri Bach is a former psychotherapist turned Life Transitional Coach. She helps women over fifty who have experienced a major life transition reclaim their spark and discover what's next. Teri supports and guides women to create that same kind of transformation, starting with the retreats she offers.

untappedpotentialcoaching.com

STOP NETWORKING, START SIGNALING

DR. LYNN BANIS

If visibility is currency, most people are still trading in expired coupons. They chase coffees, cling to conferences, and collect business cards like it's 2004. All in the name of "networking."

But here's the truth: Networking is dead. Or at least the old version of it is. You don't need to "get in the room" when your ideas can walk in before you. That's the power of signaling. Signaling is visibility with precision. It's how the right people find you, trust you, and want to work with you—before you ever speak. And unlike networking, signaling scales. One powerful piece of content can do what a hundred awkward handshakes never will.

Let's break down the shift.

Traditional networking was built for a different era. When access was limited, you had to shake hands to be seen. But today? Attention is democratized. Your smartest signal can outwork your strongest connection. Still, people cling to networking because it feels safe. Structured. Familiar. You know what's risky? Putting your ideas online. Writing a thread. Posting a bold opinion. That takes guts. But that's also what builds magnetism.

When you signal, you're not chasing opportunities. You're attracting them. You're sending out a bat-signal that says, "Here's who I am, what I believe, and how I solve problems." The people who resonate will lean in. The ones who don't? Let them scroll by.

Let's look at how signaling works in the real world. Take Jenna, a coach who used to spend hours attending events, passing out cards, and making small talk that led nowhere. One day she posted a breakdown of her signature coaching framework on LinkedIn. It wasn't polished. But it was honest, clear, and useful. Within forty-eight hours, she had three new inquiries. Within a month, she landed a corporate client. That one post outperformed a year of "networking."

Or consider Michael, a software engineer who started sharing quick videos breaking down complex coding problems. He wasn't chasing likes—he was showing how he thinks. Fast-forward three months, and he's being invited to speak on panels, mentor junior developers, and consult on projects he didn't even apply for. That's not a fluke. That's signaling at work.

Here's how to start:

First, define your signal. What do you want to be known for? What's the conversation you want to own? Get crystal clear. Then package it in ways that travel: content, ideas, visuals, frameworks. Think of your content like breadcrumbs that lead people to your doorstep.

Start with small, consistent efforts. A weekly post. A short video. A carousel slide. You don't need a content empire. You need a content fingerprint—something unique and recognizable. When people start saying, "This sounds like you," you're on the right track.

Next, show up consistently. Not just when you need something. Signal daily, weekly, rhythmically. Become a presence. Not a pop-in. Momentum matters. Each signal stacks. Each signal compounds. Visibility is not a viral event—it's a long game of trust and recall.

And then, engage like a human. Respond to comments. Join conversations. Reference others. Signal isn't a one-way transmission—it's a beacon that invites dialogue. The smartest signalers know how to listen louder than they speak. They amplify others. They build goodwill. They stay top-of-mind by being top-of-heart.

Here's the difference: Networking asks, "Who can I meet today?" Signaling asks, "How can I be seen *every* day?" Networking depends on luck and access. Signaling is a system. It works while you sleep. It works while you're off-grid. It works because it's not about you—it's about the value you consistently create.

You know who does this well? Creators who become category leaders. Think of the marketing strategist who turns bite-sized insights into binge-worthy threads. Or the designer whose Instagram showcases behind-the-scenes process instead of perfect portfolios. Or the founder who shares transparent updates on building their business. These people aren't "networking." They're building ecosystems around their ideas.

Another example is Rachel, a grief counselor who started sharing simple, heartfelt reflections about the grief process. Not academic. Not overly produced. Just real. Within six months, she wasn't just helping people—she was being featured on podcasts, asked to collaborate on a book, and had a waiting list for her services. She didn't network her way in. She signaled.

Let's zoom out. The future belongs to those who know how to broadcast signal in a noisy world. The trust economy rewards those who show up with clarity and frequency. If you've got something worth sharing—and you do!—then sharing it is your obligation.

Don't wait to be invited. Don't wait to be introduced. Don't wait until your brand is perfect or your framework is flawless. Start now, start rough, and refine in public. That's where the growth lives.

And remember, your signal doesn't have to be loud to be powerful. Some of the most effective signals are quiet, deeply thoughtful, and consistent. It's not about making noise. It's about creating resonance. When your voice aligns with your values, people don't just hear you—they feel you.

Because here's the quiet irony: The best networkers today aren't "networking" at all. They're signaling so clearly that others are networking *with them*.

The best part? When you start signaling instead of networking, you flip the dynamic. You stop begging for attention and start commanding it. You stop asking for a seat at the table and start building your own. Visibility isn't about being everywhere. It's about being unmistakable where it matters.

So stop networking. Start signaling. Because signaling is the lighthouse in a foggy harbor. It doesn't chase the ships—it guides them in. It doesn't demand attention—it earns it through clarity, consistency, and trust. Your voice, when steady and true, becomes the beacon. Let it shine. Whether you're sharing your story on a podcast, speaking at a local business meetup, leading a breakout session at a regional conference, or commanding the main stage at an international summit, each moment builds your signal. From intimate living room talks to virtual summits with global reach, every stage—no matter how small—magnifies your message. Each signal strengthens your lighthouse. Speak with clarity. Share with intention. And watch what happens when the right people start coming to you.

Dr. Lynn Banis transforms profound loss into powerful new beginnings. After losing her mother, brother, and husband in three years, she developed a proven approach to help women reclaim purpose, redesign life, and live with joy. She guides clients from heartbreak to wholeness with wisdom, clarity, and compassion.

app.widowsrisingtogether.com

WHEN SILENCE SPEAKS: RECLAIMING YOUR VOICE IN THE WORKPLACE

SALLY BENDERSKY

S ometimes, *silence is eloquent.* It happens in meetings, in conversations, in moments when you speak and no one responds. You share an idea, and there are no questions or comments from the people in the room. Minutes later, someone repeats it, and suddenly everyone agrees it is brilliant. You wonder: *Did I say it wrong? Was I too quiet? Or too bold?*

I've been there. I've felt that kind of silence more than once. And I've learned that it didn't mean I was wrong. It meant something deeper is at play. This story is about one of those moments, and what triggered me to learn about mindset, presence, voice, and the power of visibility.

The Meeting That Changed Me

Years ago, I was working in a bank, in the Information Technology Division, preparing a proposal for a new initiative. I spent days crafting it until I thought it was clear, structured, and backed by data. I was proud of it. What I liked most was that it would simplify the lives of our clients. I walked into the meeting, the only woman in the room, and presented my idea with confidence. Then . . . nothing. No questions. No comments. Just silence.

But as the meeting went on, I heard my proposal again, coming from other people in the room. They repeated the ideas I had presented, sometimes with the same words, as fresh propositions of their own. I sat there, stunned. I had done the work, and my presentation was clear enough to stimulate two or three people in the audience to claim that they were presenting innovative ideas. I was invisible in that room.

That moment did not break me. It woke me up. I realized there was a strong correlation between my invisibility and the fact that I was the only woman in that group.

The Label That Followed

Shortly after the meeting, I found out that some colleagues, and even my boss, called me "conflictive" behind my back. I tried to understand, because I was always particularly cautious not to hurt anyone and to maintain a very professional presence. I believed it should be easy to see how deeply I cared about our work. And I was also enthusiastic when presenting my ideas. I showed personal initiative, vision, conviction, and clarity. I thought these were highly regarded qualities for employees. But I was wrong. They were important only for male professionals.

This was hurtful. I knew that if a man had spoken the same way, he would have been called a leader.

Trying to understand my position in the company, I started talking to a few other professional women at the bank. I could only find a handful. Most of them had comparable stories. They had been overlooked, dismissed, or quietly labeled as "difficult" for simply showing up with strength. It became clear that it wasn't just about me. It was a pattern. And once I saw it, I couldn't help thinking I should do something about it. The situation for professional women in the workplace was hard, and people did not realize it. Although it hurt to be called "conflictive," I knew that my difficulties in being visible did not stem from aggression but from lack of awareness due to the way in which women are brought up in our society.

This wasn't all. I discovered that a few men in our division were also invisible. I remember a conversation with Patrick, a colleague in my office. I was telling him that women were discriminated against in the bank to the point of disappearing. I stressed that I could prove this since I had talked to almost all the female professionals who worked in our large building, and they all felt discriminated against. He responded by saying that we live in a culture that equates leadership with assertiveness, whereas he was an introvert who disliked showing off, and his leadership style was empathetic and collaborative. He didn't rush people into doing tasks without knowing that they understood what he was asking and why. This caused him to be often overlooked. He said, "I didn't know that being considerate of others could make me disappear." It became clear to me that visibility is not only a matter of gender. It's also about how we show up, and how others have been taught to respond.

Learning to Be Seen

After the meeting, I realized that invisibility affected my mood. I felt diminished, empty, as if a vacuum cleaner had sucked all the energy out of me. It took me a couple of weeks of reflection to overcome my mood and recover my usual energy, and when I did, I decided that I would no longer be invisible. I would learn how to be seen and spare everyone from feeling my "conflictive behavior." I would insist on being clear, intentional, present, and at the same time, as gentle as I possibly could be.

I started framing my ideas differently. I documented my work. I wasn't the first to start conversations at meetings. First, I listened to and supported my colleagues, and when I did speak, there were always one or two who supported me.

Visibility became a skill that I practiced every day.

The Story Goes On

Because of my decision to gain visibility and due to the daily practice that followed, I started to think differently about my life and what I wanted it to be. Things began to change. The days of reflection had done their work. I realized that I needed to think bigger. I had created my own barriers from my experience about how the world works and my belief that I needed to adapt to it, regardless of my suffering. Not long after that important meeting, I got married, left the bank, and created my own consulting company, sharing it with my husband, who consulted in a different field. I stopped working in Information Technology and offered my services in strategy, organizational development, and management, which I considered my professional strengths. Soon after, I became a coach and created, together with my instructors, the first-ever school of professional coaching in the Spanish language, with students participating from seven different countries in Ibero-America. I was CEO, sales manager, producer, and, together with my two partners, a supervisor of the students' learning process.

This was a very intense experience, and a great one. I became extremely visible, for better and for worse. Although it proved to be very successful in the end, there were quite a few breakdowns during the process, and I was held responsible for each one because I was the CEO. I was so thrilled being where I was that I took on every one of them as a project with issues that needed to be solved. I have no doubt that this attitude, which I maintain to this day for any kind of breakdown in my life, led to the success of this adventure, which was the first step of Ibero-American professional coaching—a field that continued developing at high speed.

I was never again a nonexistent entity in my professional field. That is how I came to have important positions in diverse areas of action, like executive director of a state technology development center, where I was elected among more than one hundred applicants from around the world, including Chile; ambassador of Chile in Israel for six years, named by the president of Chile; Ministerial Secretary of Higher Education, selected and named by the Minister of Education; plus president of boards of important institutions like public ports. I had become a visible public figure in my country.

Would You Like to Be Visible?

Visibility isn't about ego. It's about respect. It's about making sure your ideas, your work, and your leadership are recognized and valued in every space you enter. It's not something you're born with; it's something you build. How? By widening your mindset, showing your presence, letting your voice be heard, and, step-by-step, experiencing the power of visibility by practicing, practicing, practicing.

And it's not just for you. When you show up fully, you make space for others to do the same. You shift the room. You change the culture.

Last Words

If you've ever felt invisible, I want you to know that you're not alone. You're not wrong. Your voice matters. Your presence matters. And your story isn't over. To be visible, you don't need to be loud. You must just be clear. You must just be you.

Let your silence speak, and then let your voice follow.

Sally Bendersky, visionary leader and bestselling author, is a transformative leadership coach renowned for empowering executives worldwide. With a distinguished career as ambassador and CEO, and now president of the Chilean Academy of Engineering, she inspires leaders to excel and organizations to thrive through her bold leadership and deep expertise.

sallybcoach.com

WHO KNEW VISION BOARDS
REALLY WORKED?

Elizabeth Bennett

I 'll be honest with you: For the longest time, I thought vision boards were a little "woo-woo."

Pretty pictures. Clever words. A collage taped together from magazines. Could something like that really change anything in my life?

But then, one afternoon, I found myself surrounded by a mountain of torn-out pages from travel, lifestyle, and business magazines, searching for messages that would push me to act differently, make braver decisions, and imagine myself in a bigger life than I'd ever dared to speak out loud.

That was the moment I stopped seeing vision boards as crafts—and started treating them as commitments.

The Early Boards

My first attempt was small: a poster board tucked into the corner of my walk-in closet. The words and images stared back at me for years, but I didn't engage with them. I didn't breathe life into the pictures, and they eventually became background noise. When I moved, I packed the tattered board away, wondering if it was even worth keeping.

But something in me wasn't ready to give up.

The second attempt was bigger, bolder—an enormous trifold display I plastered with photographs of Africa, the front end of a Mercedes Benz, children from different nations, symbols of wealth, postcards of sunny destinations, and words that spoke to dreams I'd never confessed to anyone else.

That board wasn't hidden in a closet. I hung it on the wall with duct tape, where I saw it daily. I didn't just look at it—I really spoke to it. I imagined myself inside those pictures. I practiced seeing myself living that life.

Still, I didn't fully believe. Not yet.

A Turning Point

The real shift came during a workshop with a group of entrepreneurs. The facilitator handed each of us a small corkboard, explaining that it was meant to sit on our desks so we'd see it every single day.

At first, I laughed. "How am I supposed to fit all my dreams on something this small?"

She smiled knowingly and told me to just *start*.

As I searched through the materials she had provided, one phrase leapt off the page and shook me:

"Tell your stories. Own everything that has happened to you. Don't leave anything out. It's all good stuff."

I can still feel the jolt of recognition. It was as if the Universe itself had written those words just for me. For the first time, I understood that visibility wasn't just about what I wanted in the future—it was also about honoring every part of my past.

I glued that phrase at the very center of my board. Around it, I arranged calligraphy words written by the facilitator's daughter, alongside images and symbols that spoke to my soul.

When I carried that board home, I felt different. Energized. Committed. Visible—at least to myself.

The Proof

Not long after, I pulled out all three of my vision boards — the dusty first attempt, the trifold masterpiece, and the small corkboard that carried such power.

For the first time, I really looked at them.

And what I saw left me speechless.

WIRED FOR WONDER: THRIVING WITH ADULT ADHD

CAROLYN CAHN

A DHD isn't a character flaw or a lack of discipline; it's a neurodevelopmental condition that affects how the brain regulates attention, impulses, and executive function. For adults living with ADHD, the experience often feels like having a brain wired for fireworks in a world built for candlelight. Traits like distractibility, impulsivity, hyperfocus, and emotional intensity aren't signs of weakness; they're reflections of a brain that processes stimulation and reward differently.

Neurologically, ADHD is linked to lower dopamine levels and altered activity in the prefrontal cortex, the part of the brain responsible for planning, decision-making, and impulse control. This isn't about being "lazy" or "forgetful"; it's about how the brain prioritizes and responds to information. ADHD isn't a deficit of attention; it's a dysregulation of it. The brain doesn't struggle to pay attention; it struggles to regulate what it pays attention to, when, and for how long.

Many adults with ADHD go undiagnosed for years. Their symptoms are often mislabeled as laziness, anxiety, or depression. It's important to note that often secondary diagnoses might exist with a person diagnosed with ADHD.

People with ADHD often face additional challenges. More than 50 percent of people with ADHD have a secondary or co-occurring diagnoses that can include depression, anxiety, obsessive-compulsive disorder (OCD), bipolar disorder, and learning disorders such as dyslexia. In addition, many sources have identified that more than 50 percent of those with ADHD also have addictive personalities that can result in behaviors leading to alcohol or drug abuse, compulsive hoarding, gambling, or internet or video game addictions.

While each person has a unique set of challenges, we see some more frequently in the ADHD community. Time blindness makes it hard to estimate how long tasks will take. Starting or finishing projects can feel like climbing a mountain with no map. Emotional dysregulation leads to intense reactions, while sensory overload can make everyday environments feel overwhelming. Distractibility and difficulty focusing also play roles in making life more challenging. Even simple tasks like choosing what to wear or responding to an email can feel paralyzing when one's executive function is compromised.

These challenges ripple into relationships, careers, and self-esteem. Missed deadlines, forgotten appointments, and misunderstood intentions can create a cycle of guilt, frustration, and strained relationships. But these struggles aren't signs of failure; they're signs of a brain that needs different tools. If you have ADHD, you're not broken. You're simply navigating a world that wasn't built for your wiring. And once you understand that, everything begins to shift.

ADHD is more than a list of challenges; it's also a constellation of strengths. Adults with ADHD often possess extraordinary creativity, generating ideas others might never consider. Their ability to hyperfocus allows them to dive deeply into tasks they're passionate about, producing work of remarkable depth and quality. When engaged, they can work with laser-like intensity, often losing track of time in the best way.

Empathy is another gift—many with ADHD feel emotions intensely and connect deeply with others. They're often the ones who notice when someone's mood shifts, offer support without being asked, and bring emotional depth to their relationships. And resilience? It's practically a superpower. Navigating life with ADHD requires constant adaptation, and that builds grit, flexibility, and courage. ADHD minds are often the ones asking, "What if?" and changing the world because of it.

Receiving an ADHD diagnosis in adulthood can be transformative. It's not just a label—it's a lens that brings your life into focus. Suddenly, past struggles make sense. The missed deadlines, emotional swings, and chaotic mornings weren't personal failures; they were symptoms of an unrecognized condition. Being diagnosed with ADHD can feel like a homecoming—a moment when your life story finally has a coherent narrative. It's an answer to all the challenges you've faced through the years that negatively altered your view of yourself and the world around you.

To get diagnosed, consult a psychiatrist or psychologist who specializes in adult ADHD. The emotional impact of diagnosis often includes relief, grief, and validation. Relief that there's an explanation. Grief for the years spent struggling. And validation that your experience is real. Diagnosis is the beginning of understanding, not the end. What's important is the steps you take once you have a diagnosis. Your family, friends, and workplace will have beneficial outcomes based upon how you choose to move forward with your information.

For those who were diagnosed earlier in life, symptoms may evolve over time. Hormonal shifts, life stressors, and changing environments can all influence how ADHD presents. Symptoms can change or vary over time. Every person has their own unique experience and coping mechanisms. What works for one adult may not work for another, and that's okay. ADHD is not a one-size-fits-all condition, and neither is its management.

Living with ADHD means building systems that support your unique brain. Time management tools like visual timers, alarms, and time-blocking on your calendar can help anchor your day. Breaking tasks into micro-steps makes them less overwhelming, and body doubling—working alongside someone else—can boost motivation. These tools aren't just helpful; they're often essential. Having accountability partners, joining ADHD groups, and having a coach can all be beneficial.

Organizational strategies should be visual and tactile: color coding, open shelving, and regular decluttering. If you can see it, you're more likely to remember it. Emotional regulation can be supported through mindfulness, journaling, breathing techniques, and other grounding practices. These aren't rigid rules; they're scaffolding for your brilliance. Structure isn't restriction; it's liberation. It's the framework that allows your creativity and energy to flourish.

ADHD can shape how you connect with others. Interrupting, forgetfulness, and emotional reactivity can strain relationships, but awareness and communication transforms them. Practicing active listening, using reminders for important dates, and being open about your needs help build trust and understanding. Relationships thrive when you lead with honesty, curiosity, and compassion for yourself and for others.

Support systems like therapy, ADHD coaches, and peer groups offer guidance and connection. There's power in being seen and understood. ADHD coaching can provide practical strategies tailored to your lifestyle, while therapy can help unpack emotional patterns and build resilience. Connection thrives when we lead with honesty and curiosity. You don't have to do this alone.

Adults with ADHD often shine in careers that are dynamic, creative, or high-pressure. Roles such as entrepreneur, artist, emergency responder, teacher, or tech innovator allow for flexibility, stimulation, and impact. The key is finding environments that align with your strengths. You may thrive in roles others find chaotic because your brain is wired to handle complexity and rapid change.

To increase productivity, use noise-canceling headphones, schedule regular breaks, and set alarms to manage both work and rest time. Don't hesitate to advocate for special accommodations when necessary. As an example, this might be beneficial if sitting in a room with others for an examination creates concentration challenges because you are easily distracted by noises. Many workplaces offer flexibility when asked, and keep in mind that your needs are valid. Many successful figures, including Simone Biles, Richard Branson, Justin Timberlake, Will Smith, and Michael Phelps, have ADHD. Your brain isn't a barrier—it's a blueprint for innovation.

Because ADHD often coexists with other mental health and behavioral challenges, managing your mental health is essential. Therapy, medication when appropriate, and lifestyle changes can make a profound difference. But just as important is cultivating self-compassion. You are not your productivity. You are not your to-do list.

Forgive missed deadlines. Celebrate small wins. Reframe setbacks as data—not verdicts. You're not failing—you're learning. And healing isn't linear—it's layered, personal, and powerful. You're allowed to be a work in progress and a masterpiece at the same time. Progress isn't always visible, but it's always valuable.

You don't have to navigate ADHD alone. There are a wide range of providers who can help. Psychiatrists and psychologists can assist with diagnosis and medication management. Therapists offer emotional support and coping strategies. ADHD coaches provide practical tools and accountability. When selecting someone, research them to ensure they are experienced in working with adult ADHD. The right support can make all the difference.

Books like *ADHD Is Your Superpower: Harness Your Unique Mind for Success*, cell phone apps, and ADHD communities locally or on the internet offer connection and insight. Podcasts, YouTube channels, and online courses can also provide education and encouragement.

Community turns struggle into strength. Shared experience turns isolation into empowerment.

ADHD doesn't define your limits—it reveals your potential. Success isn't linear. It's built on adaptation, creativity, and grit. Your story matters—your challenges, your triumphs, your voice. Keep going. The world needs your perspective. The way your brain works isn't a mistake; it's a masterpiece in motion.

You're not too much. You're exactly enough. And you're just getting started.

As a seasoned success coach and registered nurse, **Carolyn Cahn** has more than thirty-five years of experience empowering adults to transform their lives. With advanced degrees and certifications in NLP, coaching, IEMT and hypnosis, she helps individuals tackle low self-esteem, procrastination, poor time management, ADHD, and burnout, guiding them toward personal and professional fulfillment.

carolyncahn.com

START SMART, SCALE STRONG: VISIBILITY TO THE SIMPLE TECHNOLOGY EVERY NEW BUSINESS NEEDS

EARLENE COATS

The Moment That Changed Everything

I had just checked into a hotel room in Oklahoma City when my phone rang. It was my daughter—she was in labor and on the way to the hospital. I would miss the birth of my first grandchild. I wasn't supposed to travel to Oklahoma City that week, but an "urgent" meeting came up. In that moment, I reflected on all the significant events I had missed out on because of my nine-to-five job.

That was the day I chose to step out in faith and begin a new journey. I didn't know exactly what it would look like, but I knew I wanted a business that gave me freedom, not chains. A business aligned with who God created me to be.

I wish I could tell you it was a straight path to overnight success, but that would only mislead you. Through my missteps, God was very patient with me and helped ease me back on track.

Lessons from My Journey

- **Don't Be Drawn in by Easy Promises**

  What looks simple on the surface—like "plug-and-play" opportunities—often leads to frustration if it's not in alignment with your God-given path. Discern whether the business is truly yours to build before jumping in.

- **Choose Leaders Who Reflect Your Values**

  The voices you follow will shape your journey. Surround yourself with mentors and leaders who share your faith, values, and vision so you're not pulled off course by someone else's agenda.

- **Build the Business God Called You to, Not Someone Else's**

  Copying someone else's blueprint may look like a shortcut, but it keeps you from walking in the unique assignment God placed on your life. Stay anchored in the mission He gave you.

- **Invest in Tools at the Right Time**

  Buying every "must-have" tool too early only creates overwhelm. Instead, focus on mastering the season you're in and add tools as your business grows.

- **Pursue God's Goals, Not Borrowed Ones**

  True success comes when your goals are aligned with God's purpose for you—not when you chase numbers or milestones that look impressive but aren't rooted in your calling.

Steps to Gain Clarity on Your Calling

I love the Stephen Covey quote, "Begin with the end in mind." This can be applied to many areas of our lives. As you start your business, it is a critical first step.

Some great questions to help you gain clarity on what the end might be are:

- What are some of the forgotten dreams God put on your heart?
- What has God called you to?

- What unique gifting has He placed in you?
- Whom are you called to serve?
- What is your purpose and passion?

Next consider the obstacles/roadblocks that have kept you from pursuing your dreams or calling. The obstacles may be the fear of leaving the "security" of your job, limiting beliefs, or lies you have believed based on what others have told you.

Overcome those obstacles by writing down everything you're grateful for. You may have to start with something as simple as the pen you are writing with, or the chair you are sitting on. Soon the ideas will be flowing!

Your mind is now ready to start looking for possible solutions. Ask yourself empowering questions and start listing everything that comes to you. Consider writing them in one of these formats: "I am grateful . . ." or "I am grateful in advance for . . ." Ask yourself:

1. What steps can I take to revive my dream today?
2. What's one bold move I can take today toward my vision? What's stopping me from taking that step?
3. If I knew I couldn't fail, what's the first big step I would take? What's one small action I will take today to move me closer?

Once you are clear on those answers, it's time to start discussing the tools. Technology should support your calling, not dictate it.

The Trap of Shiny Objects

Let's be honest, there's no shortage of workshops, courses, and "must-have" platforms out there. You can attend a three-day masterclass and walk away convinced you need every tool or product presented. You may eventually need them in your business, but investing too early just costs you both time and money.

I've fallen for it myself. I'm technical. I can see how tools connect and scale. But I've learned the hard way that implementing technology too soon only creates overwhelm and waste.

The key is knowing the right tool for the right time. Start simple. Use what you need today. Build a migration plan for tomorrow. And when you're ready for the complex, you'll often also be ready to hire support to manage it.

Case Study: Spinning in Circles

One client I worked with illustrates this perfectly. She already had everything she needed to launch her workshop:

- A paid Zoom account to deliver the workshop
- Social media to promote the workshop
- A way to collect payments

She was ready to go. But instead of delivering the workshop, she spent months chasing free trial accounts, comparing products she wouldn't need for at least six month to a year down the road. She needed to be making money now, yet she was paralyzed by the "end game" and couldn't move forward with the *now game.*

By the time she came to me, she had wasted valuable time and was still stuck. Together, we refocused her: **Deliver what you have with the tools you already own.**

She launched, made money, and then we developed a roadmap for her to scale her business by adding the tools that were needed for her most time-consuming tasks. The result? Momentum, confidence, and the ability to invest her time and money in tools that supported her business instead of adding stress and overwhelm.

Putting First Things First

Here's what I've learned, both in my journey and through coaching others:

When you're starting a business, the order matters. It's not about having the fanciest tool set; it's about having the *right* one. When just starting out, you can do much of what you need with Google tools.

Four categories form the foundation:

1. **Project Management** – A simple way to organize your tasks, deadlines, and ideas. It can be sticky notes on the wall, a Google sheet, or even paper, but it must keep you moving forward.

2. **Product Delivery** – A clear method to get your product or service to clients. For many new entrepreneurs, this is Zoom, an online course platform, or even a simple download.

3. **Payment Collection** – A secure, easy way for people to pay you. Don't complicate this. Clarity and simplicity build trust.

4. **Marketing and Social Media** – One primary channel to start. You don't need to be everywhere; you need to be consistent where your people already are.

Start here. Build confidence. Then scale intentionally.

From Chaos to Clarity

The women I serve are often stuck in jobs that no longer fit, aching to build something more meaningful, but tangled in the weeds of "how." They don't need a second full-time job in the form of complicated tech. They need a path that lets them show up in *small, powerful steps.*

When they simplify their tools, the chaos falls away. They start delivering instead of overplanning. They begin serving real clients instead of sitting on unused software. They taste momentum, and that momentum births courage.

I've watched women leave their nine-to-five jobs, not because they hustled harder, but because they learned to work smarter, aligned with their gifts, and free from overwhelm.

And when they show up in this way—clear, simple, faithful— they don't just build businesses. They step into the fullness of who God created them to be.

Your Next Steps

If you're at the beginning of your journey—or maybe stuck in the middle—here's what I recommend:

1. **Pray and Plan.** Begin with the end in mind. Ask God to clarify your calling, gifts, and audience.
2. **Audit Your Tools.** What do you already have that you can use today? What's truly necessary now?
3. **Launch Simply.** Deliver your product or service with the smallest set of tools possible. Don't wait for perfect.
4. **Add with Intention.** Only bring in new technology when you've outgrown your current system—not before.
5. **Align Everything.** Make sure every step, tool, and system supports your gifts, your calling, and the life you want to live.

Closing Encouragement

I missed my granddaughter's birth because my life was run by someone else's schedule. I don't want you . . . or any of the women I serve . . . to miss the moments that matter most.

That's why I'm passionate about teaching a simple, scalable approach to technology. When you use tools in the right order, aligned with your gifts and God's vision, you gain more than visibility. You gain freedom. You gain presence. You gain the legacy you long to leave.

Start smart. Scale strong. Remember: you don't need to do it all at once. Just take the next right step. God will meet you there.

Earlene Coats is a purpose-driven business strategist who helps Christian women launch their God-centered business. Fluent in both "geek" and English, Earlene simplifies tech solutions, tailoring them to each entrepreneur's unique needs by starting with the end in mind and implementing the right solutions at the right time.

dreamupevents.com

FROM ZERO TO THOUSANDS OF DEALS: MY JOURNEY TO FREEDOM THROUGH REAL ESTATE

ROBBIE CRAGER

In late 1997, I made a decision that would alter the course of my life.

I walked away from my job.

I had no money in the bank.

My credit was wrecked.

I didn't have a backup plan or a single mentor cheering me on.

But I knew I couldn't keep living the same year on repeat and call it a future.

I was in my house late one night, flipping through TV channels, restless and frustrated. That's when I landed on a Carlton Sheets infomercial about real estate investing.

I didn't even buy the course. But I watched the testimonies of regular people—men and women who had jumped in, taken chances, and changed their lives. Something stirred in me.

I didn't have money. I didn't have credit. What I did have was a choice: keep making excuses, or step into the unknown. I decided to jump in with both feet.

The Leap

My first deal wasn't the fast success story I had pictured. I thought I'd buy a house, flip it quickly, and make an easy profit. Instead, it took years to sell.

I had to pivot from a "quick flip" into becoming a landlord, figuring out rentals on the fly. On top of that, my partners on the deal started fighting with each other. It got ugly, and I eventually had to buy them out just to keep things moving forward.

It wasn't glamorous, and it wasn't easy. But that first deal taught me lessons I could never have learned from a book or a course. I learned how to adapt when plans change, how to manage tenants and cash flow, and the importance of choosing the right partners.

And most importantly, I learned that persistence matters more than perfection.

By my second deal, things looked different. I made $14,000. That win proved I was on the right path.

The Climb

Over the years that followed, I went all in. I studied every deal structure I could find—wholesaling, fix-and-flip, buy-and-hold, seller financing, and subject-to. I learned how to get creative when banks said no, and I learned how to build partnerships that could fill in the gaps I couldn't fill on my own.

Not every deal was a home run, but I kept going. I kept learning. And step by step, I built momentum.

Fast-forward two decades, and I had bought and sold more than three thousand houses.

When you do that many deals, you see what works. The people who succeed in real estate aren't always the ones with the most money—they're the ones who take action, learn from mistakes, and surround themselves with the right people.

For a long time, I thought wholesaling was the fastest path to success. It brought in cash quickly, sure. But I realized something important: wholesaling is a job. If you stop working, the money stops too. That's not freedom.

So I shifted into **value-add investing**—buying properties where I could force equity through renovations, better management, or repositioning the use of the property. That's where true wealth is built.

The Puerto Rico Chapter

Seven years ago, I made another life-altering move: I relocated to Puerto Rico.

Most people assume it was just for tax incentives. And while the financial benefits are real, that wasn't my main reason. I saw Puerto Rico as one of the most unique real estate markets in the world—full of challenges, yes, but also full of opportunity.

The island doesn't have a functional MLS. Financing is difficult. Properties sit abandoned for years. But if you can navigate the chaos, the opportunities are tremendous.

In just seven years, my team and I have acquired more than two hundred properties on the island, investing more than $30 million and creating another $30 million in equity.

Some of my proudest moments here have been taking forgotten, abandoned buildings and turning them into housing again. Seeing families move into places the community had given up on—that's powerful.

Puerto Rico hasn't just been a business move for me. It's been deeply personal. I've built relationships with local partners, worked on projects that have real community impact, and experienced firsthand how real estate can be a tool for transformation.

The Power of Partnerships

If there's one theme running through my career, it's this: The money is not the most important part of a deal; people are.

I've worked with "rainmakers" who could find deals anywhere, operators who could manage projects with precision, and funders who could structure capital in creative ways.

And yes, I've also partnered with people who made things messy, stressful, and expensive. But those experiences taught me that choosing your partners is just as important as choosing the property itself.

That's why today I focus on creating win-win partnerships through my communities, especially Apex, where I connect serious investors to one another. Whether you're a finder, funder, or operator, the right partnership can accelerate your journey in ways you can't achieve alone.

Freedom, Legacy, and Purpose

Real estate has given me far more than financial success.

It has given me freedom—the freedom to live where I want, travel when I want, and spend my time on what matters most.

It has given me purpose—the ability to help others escape broken systems and create financial independence for themselves and their families.

And it has given me a legacy—not just in terms of properties and deals, but in the lives I've touched along the way.

That's why I started the **Flip Flop Flipper** brand. I wanted to show people that success doesn't mean wearing a suit and tie or playing by someone else's rules. You can do deals in shorts and sandals. You can build wealth while being yourself.

My mission now is simple: to help as many people as possible achieve freedom through real estate. Because if I could start with nothing—no money, no credit, no guidance—then you can too.

If you're reading this and thinking, *That sounds great, but I don't have what it takes,* let me tell you, I once thought the same thing.

The only difference between who I was in 1997 and who I am today is that I took action. I started when I didn't feel ready. I learned by doing, even when I made mistakes.

Real estate changed my life. And it can change yours too.

Stop waiting for the perfect moment. Stop waiting until everything lines up. Take the next step with what you have, right where you are.

Freedom is built one deal at a time.

Robbie Crager is a real estate investor, entrepreneur, and founder of the Flip Flop Flipper brand. With more than twenty-six years of experience, Robbie specializes in partnerships that create long-term wealth, connecting serious investors to deals, funding, and collaboration. Robbie lives in Puerto Rico and invests across both the U.S. mainland and the island.

theflipflopflipper.com

YOU DON'T NEED PERMISSION

SHARON GALLUZZO

One night I decided I was *done* waiting for someone to see me and give me permission to be successful.

Moving to a new state meant that everything was new. When we relocated, I had to create new communities and new relationships. One of the things I had done since high school was theatre, and I wanted to continue acting, so I needed to find a place to perform.

Fortunately, there were a lot of community theatres in the area, and I was excited at the idea of getting back on stage. I got up my courage, found audition notices, registered, and began preparing.

Some auditions are "monologue" auditions: You select, memorize, and perform a monologue in the allotted time. This style of audition, in my opinion, is more difficult because you rarely know what the director is actually looking for.

I accepted the risk. I dug into research to find just the right piece, memorized, it and rehearsed my buns off. The day of the audition, I felt confident and prepared. When it was my turn, I took a deep breath and jumped in. As I finished, I triumphantly waited for the director's feedback.

It. Was. Brutal. Not since college had someone been so negatively critical of my acting decisions.

"It's the wrong type of monologue," they said.

"Where did you even find that?" one of the directors chided, looking down his nose at me.

They also didn't like my acting choices. "Why did you sit down instead of stand up?"

On and on it went. I was humiliated.

I put away my dreams of getting back on stage. I gave up. I mean, I had enough to do. I had two small children and a whole new life to create.

Still, the nudge to "tread the boards" never went away. The desire to perform returned again and again.

And that's how I found myself a few years later looking once again for audition notices. This time I didn't have to go through the dreaded monologue process. This notice read, "Cold readings." That means reading excerpts from the script.

The day of the audition arrived, and I was nervous. I was also full of doubt and fear. My body actually remembered the humiliation and disappointment the last time I put myself out there. I felt sick.

Despite my fear, my desire to perform made me willing to take the risk. That desire didn't overwhelm the doubt, however. The drive to the audition was torture as those old, terrible audition memories began to haunt me. *What if it happens again?*

I replayed the past over and over in my head. I imagined all the things that might go wrong. I seriously considered turning the car around and going back home.

Sometimes (and this was one of those times), I experience sudden flashes of brilliance. Into my mind came a challenge: *What if you walked into this audition as if you belonged?*

All at once, I was in creation mode! Yes! What if I walked in like this is *my* home? What if everyone *already* knew and loved me? What if this is where I *belonged?*

I grabbed on to this inspiration like a life preserver. I repeated these ideas to myself over and over. I convinced myself that this was my new reality. *I'm here and I belong.*

As I entered the building, I took a deep breath and walked confidently up to the table. The person checking people in was super friendly, and I acted like we were old friends. I grabbed the scripts and went into a huge room full of strangers. I didn't know one single person in that room.

It was clear that most of them knew one another. Doubt crept in again.

What am I doing here?

Look, they probably already know who they want to cast.

Stop, I reminded myself. *I belong.*

The night was exciting, and I got to see lots of folks perform. I got ideas about how I wanted to read the material differently, so they would notice me. I owned my confidence. I belonged.

And it worked. Not only did I get cast in one of the plays—I found out later that the directors had fought over who got to cast me!

This was my first glimpse of **not** waiting for permission to belong, be successful, or be seen. Today I realize this lesson is key to what I teach entrepreneurs: Be visible and choose yourself instead of waiting for permission from someone else.

Transformation like this, flipping the script, defining a new reality, is an inside job. You first must claim it internally before you can step into it externally.

That deep breath I took walking into the building really wasn't about calming nerves; it was me stepping into a decision I had already made in the car: *I belong here.* You must see yourself differently first, make the decision, then walk it out.

The entrepreneurs I work with may not *think* they're waiting for permission, yet it shows up in subtle ways.

It shows up in hesitating to ask for the sale (or not asking at all). Failing to market and advertise—being the best kept secret in their field. Hiding behind busy work and not addressing the needs of the business. Giving attention to anything and everything but what needs to be done to grow their businesses.

Just as I almost turned my car around on the way to that audition, many business owners step back the precise moment when they need to step forward. They hide . . . failing to be visible to those who need the solution their businesses provide–that is, their customers.

Visibility does not begin when others see you. It begins when you decide to stop hiding.

The root cause of hiding, though, is fear. Fear of judgment. Fear of being too much. Fear of being not enough. Maybe you were told as a child that it's not polite to brag, that it's prideful to promote yourself, and pride is bad.

So you wait. I mean, who do you think you are? Here's your answer:

Who am I to be brilliant, gorgeous, talented, fabulous? Actually, who are you not to be? Your playing small does not serve. There is nothing enlightened about shrinking so that other people won't feel insecure around you. We are all meant to shine.

— Marianne Williamson

Then, what do you do with the feelings of inadequacy?

You can actually change those limiting thoughts. You (and only you) are in charge of your feelings. Since that's the case, you can choose something different.

Of course, you can't always choose the immediate feeling that occurs when something happens. However, you have the power to choose the next feeling, the next thought. When you feel scared, you can choose to feel excited instead. (Actually these two emotions feel exactly the same to the body. Your body doesn't have context for the feeling until you name it.) If frustration rears its ugly head, decide to be motivated instead. You choose if you feel angry, upset, and discontented or happy, fulfilled, and joyful.

My encouragement is to embrace your power. Give yourself permission. Choose.

Are you ready?

Here's the truth: Confidence follows as you *take action* in your *full power*, because confidence is built as you move . . . not before.

The confidence I had walking into the room full of strangers wasn't because I was certain I'd be cast in a play. It came from a decision. It came from taking the action of walking into the room anyway.

Growth and opportunity live just outside your comfort zone. What would you do if you were not waiting for permission?

Ironically, when I stopped waiting to be picked, stopped giving away my power, and acted like I already belonged, I ended up being more sought after than I imagined.

So, how do you step up and take control and be confident when you're not?

I have great news! Confidence is portable.

If you are confident in one area of your life—maybe it's running, or knitting, or designing spreadsheets, you already know how it feels to *be* confident. It's possible to take that feeling of confidence into uncomfortable or unfamiliar situations.

Your body and brain already know how to be confident. By drawing on past experiences and bringing them into the moment, embodying them, you can override the doubt and fear that keep you stuck, hidden, and invisible.

It comes down to this: You can choose to wait, to hide, to be invisible—or you can choose to walk in like you belong. Because you do.

Sharon Galluzzo's mission is to unleash the full potential of entrepreneurs to create successful businesses that make a positive impact on our world. She helps business and franchise owners build rock-solid businesses with consistent sales and sustainable growth. Sharon is a Profit Growth Strategist, international speaker, author, and host of *The Profit Connections Podcast*.

sharongalluzzo.com

REKINDLING VISIBILITY: CHOOSING TO BE FULLY ALIVE AFTER FIFTY

SHARON H. GIST

I know what it feels like to be visible. My life has been marked by moments when I stood out, broke ground, and opened doors that hadn't been opened before. From pioneering programs for children with special needs as a young public-school teacher, to speaking in sixty-seven cities and meeting with more than twenty-five hundred people while helping grow a financial firm from $3 million to $17 billion in assets, visibility has been woven into my story. It hasn't always been easy, but it has always been transformative.

And I also know what it feels like to become invisible.

For the past five years, my life's spotlight shifted from stages, classrooms, and boardrooms to living rooms and hospital rooms. I became a full-time caregiver for my sisters. First, I lived with Lydia, who was ninety years old. For three years, we shared daily life together—laughs, meals, gentle moments of care—and when she transitioned, she did so with grace and happiness. That time with her was a gift for both of us.

Then I turned my care toward two of my other sisters. The last two years have been marked by doctors' appointments, dementia care,

67

and the daily work of keeping them comfortable and safe. My sister Vici, once a powerhouse saleswoman whose energy lit up rooms, has felt invisible for years. Long before dementia set in, she began to lose her sense of identity and purpose. Watching her experience of fading visibility has been painful, and yet it has also lit within me a fire: a reminder that visibility matters.

Why Visibility Matters

Visibility is not vanity. It's vitality.

When we choose to be visible, we choose to step into aliveness, no matter our age, challenges, or circumstances. For older women especially, the cultural script often whispers that we should step aside, grow quiet, or fade into the background. But I believe this is exactly the time when we should step forward. We carry wisdom, resilience, humor, love, and an irreplaceable depth of life experience. To withhold that, to stay hidden, is to rob the world of our gifts— and to rob ourselves of the joy of contribution.

For me, rebuilding visibility through speaking, networking, and building my Six Figure Elevated Entrepreneur program has been more than a business move. It has been a reclamation of myself. I'm approaching eighty years old, and yet, when I step on stage, share my message with women entrepreneurs over fifty, and watch their eyes light up with recognition and possibility, I feel more alive than ever.

Overcoming the Stories That Keep Us Hidden

I could have chosen a different story for myself.

I could have said:

- "I'm too old."
- "I can't take care of my family and build a business at the same time."
- "Technology is moving too fast—I'll never keep up."

But I didn't.

Instead, I chose to face every obstacle with faith, creativity, and a refusal to believe the lie that my best years were behind me. I chose to see caregiving not as a detour from life, but as part of the fabric of my purpose. I chose to believe that visibility is a choice, not a stage of life that expires with age.

And because I made those choices, I now stand in front of women—many of them weary, many of them stuck in stories of limitation—and I get to say, "If I can do this, so can you."

One powerful reminder of this came when I was at a three-day event where we were invited to participate in a speaking contest. There were 180 participants, but only sixteen of us applied and were accepted. I was surrounded by experienced, powerful speakers . . . and I chose to step out and claim my spot. To my delight, I won the first round, speaking for two minutes on a random topic. Day two, we were given random slides to weave into a talk of our choosing— and what fun it was to play full out and win again! Day three, we got to choose our title and talk to give in three minutes. Although I didn't win that last round, the experience of claiming my place among these extraordinary leaders reminded me that I do have a place—we all do. We all have a place to stand up and make a lasting impact. We get to integrate our lifetime of experience into a meaningful legacy.

From Caregiving to Coaching

My program, the Six Figure Elevated Entrepreneur, was born in the middle of these caregiving years. Building it has been my way of stepping back into visibility—not only for myself, but for the women who are meant to walk this path with me. My clients are women entrepreneurs over fifty who feel stuck. Their businesses may have plateaued. Their energy may be waning. They may feel invisible in a world that celebrates youth and speed.

But they are extraordinary. They carry decades of wisdom. They are ready to give more impact to the world. And they are my people.

Through coaching, I help them clear the inner blocks that keep them invisible. We dismantle the limiting beliefs—"I'm too tired," "It's too late," or "No one sees me." We then build a fresh strategic plan, grounded in joy, peace, and profit. The result? These women rekindle their businesses, their income, and most importantly, their enthusiasm for life.

Visibility is contagious. As I model it, they claim it. As they claim it, their clients and communities feel the ripple effect.

The Power of Stages

One of the most powerful ways I have reignited my own visibility has been through speaking. Getting back on stages—both in-person and virtual—has reminded me of something essential: the human connection of being seen, heard, and celebrated.

I remember the thrill of those early years in my career. At the time, I didn't know that the skills I was sharpening—the listening, the storytelling, the encouragement—would one day become the foundation for helping women entrepreneurs discover their own voices.

Now, every time I stand before an audience of women entrepreneurs over fifty, I feel the same spark. Their heads nod. Their notebooks open. Their hearts awaken as I remind them: "Your story matters. Your wisdom matters. You are not done yet. In fact, you are just getting started."

Living from Alignment

When fear creeps in—as it still does—I remember what keeps me steady: alignment.

I know that when my vision is clear, when I believe in it, and when I anchor myself in the faith that I am not alone, I can move forward with joy and peace. I live from a state of love and gratitude, and that state is my compass. It reminds me that how I relate to any issue is more important than the issue itself.

Yes, technology is moving quickly. Yes, caregiving is demanding. Yes, my body sometimes reminds me that I am nearly eighty. But none of these things define me. What defines me is the alignment I choose each day—the choice to stand visible, to serve, to love, to speak, and to create impact.

An Invitation to Visibility

If you are a woman reading this and you have felt invisible, I want to speak directly to you.

Maybe you have been caregiving, and your own dreams have been on pause.
Maybe your business feels stagnant, and you wonder if the spark can return.
Maybe you've told yourself you're too old, too tired, or too late.

I want you to know: You are not done.

Visibility is not about having a spotlight or building a massive audience. It's about choosing, every day, to bring your full self forward. It is about showing up to your own life, your own business, and your own relationships with a spirit of aliveness.

The moment you do, things shift. Enthusiasm returns. Opportunities arise. People respond to your energy. And most importantly, you begin to feel like yourself again—the vibrant, wise, unstoppable woman you always were.

Full Circle

As I look back on my life, I see a full circle. I see the young woman pioneering programs for children who had been overlooked. I see the professional standing on stages across the country, building a thriving business. I see the caregiver, sitting quietly with her sisters, making the invisible visible in the most intimate way. And I see the entrepreneur, nearly eighty years old, choosing once again to rise, to speak, to coach, and to lead.

This is the gift of visibility. It is not about ego. It is about service. It is about aliveness. It is about legacy.

And it is available to all of us—at any age, in any circumstance.

Sharon H. Gist, a transformational mentor and coach, empowers her clients through the Elevated Entrepreneur Pathway, a proven system to build sustainable, 24/7 income streams, reignite passion, and craft a joyful, abundant life. Her guidance transforms setbacks into stepping stones, ensuring that every client is equipped to achieve their dreams with confidence and clarity.

THE EMBODIED PATH

HEATHER JONES

It was a quiet morning in our bedroom. The kind of quiet that should've felt soft, maybe even romantic.

But it didn't.

I was lying on my back, eyes open, body still. He was next to me. Close. Reaching. Wanting. His touch was gentle. His intention clear. He wanted connection.

But my body ... didn't. Not out of rejection—but out of absence. I wasn't there. Not in the moment. Not in my body. Not in myself.

All I could feel was the pressure of expectation. His need. My failure. The dissonance between what was supposed to feel ... and what my body refused to welcome.

Why can't I be present?
Why does this feel like obligation instead of intimacy?
What the hell is wrong with me?

I loved him; that was never the question. But I didn't know how to access the part of me that used to enjoy reaching for him.

So I stayed still. Silent, yet so loud. Frozen, yet so unsettled. Calculating when it would be acceptable to pull away. I was just surviving — in a body I couldn't feel, in a moment I couldn't inhabit.

This intimacy? It was just another moment in a long list of to-dos. My mind was already halfway through the day: meetings, groceries, client calls, the dog, the dishwasher. I had every hour mentally filled, every detail queued. His hand on my hip didn't stand a chance against the day's plan in my brain.

Nothing in our life moved unless I moved it. When the house needed cleaning, I rallied the troops. When the garage needed organizing, I initiated it. I coordinated birthdays, holidays, vacations, school events. I planned. I executed. I led.

Everyone relied on me.

But no one saw the cost.

I was exhausted. Resentful. Righteous. Trapped in a role that looked powerful on the outside but felt suffocating on the inside.

And if I handed anything off, I couldn't trust it would be done right. Or on time. Or the way I needed it to be "done."

There's a twisted "safety" in controlling everything.

You believe that if you don't loosen your grip, nothing can break. But that same grip is a choke hold on your joy, your connection, your peace.

Even in business, I couldn't let go. No one I hired ever did it right. No one stayed. Or maybe . . . I never gave them the chance. I became the bottleneck in my own empire. My marriage. My parenting. My breath.

The Transition

A transition for me didn't happen all at once. It started with one brutal truth: We wanted the same life. We just had different stops along the way.

He wanted presence. I wanted a purpose and destination. But what I realized that morning, lying next to him, was that I had been choosing either/or when life was inviting me into both/and.

I wasn't just afraid of him letting me down. I was afraid of facing what I might feel if I stopped long enough to be still, if I stopped long enough to hear the loud silence speak to me.

I had mistaken control for safety. And strategy for strength.
But real strength?

Real strength is trust.

Trusting that I could let go and the world wouldn't collapse.
Trusting that others could do it..
Trusting that my marriage could hold me.
Trusting that I could be deeply powerful and feminine at the same time.

As I walked deeper into this process of releasing, trusting, letting go, I realized if I was reclaiming my power, I had to also release my grip on his. Without even realizing it, I had groomed the man I loved and respected into someone safe for me.

I didn't do it maliciously. I did it methodically. Quietly. Over years. I needed reliability, predictability, and trust. And instead of asking or receiving, I shaped him.

He learned what kept me calm. What kept the peace. He adapted. But in doing so, he lost the fire I fell in love with. I didn't want a man who asked permission to buy me flowers — and yet, that's exactly what I had shaped. A man who double-checked before reaching. Who waited for signals before stepping in. Who adapted to the quiet tension I carried. But what I truly longed for?

To be surprised by the sweet scent of flowers as he walked through the door.
To be met with a kiss that made me feel chosen.
To lean into arms that didn't ask for permission—they simply held.

And I had to un-groom him for him to be that again.

One day, I told my mentor, "I'm letting him choose."

He paused and challenged me. "Let him? You're still in control."

And he was right. Even in surrender, I was still scripting the terms. If I didn't allow it, it wouldn't happen. I was still the gatekeeper—still calling the shots under the guise of softness.

What would it look like if he chose . . . and I followed?

Not because I was powerless, but because I was rooted enough in my feminine to trust—his choices and mine.

That weekend, he chose to plan everything.

He booked the Airbnb. He chose a Red Room (of all the places...) — bold, sensual, alive.

And for the first time in years, I received my husband.

Not the man I shaped. The man *he* chose to be.

He led. I followed.

Not out of obligation. Not because I was less powerful.

But because I was finally safe enough to trust myself to handle all situations.

Safe Enough to Trust

How did I become safe enough to trust myself? It was a series of seeds planted along my healing journey.

That weekend cracked me open in a way no retreat ever had. The shift didn't come from a spreadsheet or a journal prompt. It came from inside my body. I paused—fully. I stopped gripping. I let the breath come in, long and slow.

And I felt something I hadn't felt in years: safety. Not intellectual safety. Not circumstantial safety. **Cellular safety. The safety only the loud silence truly feels.** It felt like a warm Arizona breeze in early summer. My stomach softened, my jaw unhooked, and for the first time in years, my breath dropped all the way down. My mind went still—not empty but peaceful—and my body no longer felt like something to manage . . . it felt like home.

But more than anything, it was the absence of what kept me stuck before. No anxiety. No stress. No pressure.

Just presence.

In learning to protect myself from pain, I had accidentally muted joy. Now, for the first time in years, I could feel both. And it was enough.

That moment in the red room wasn't a fluke. It was the fruit of my healing. And it only happened because I was finally ready.

In my twenties, I was groomed and sexually abused by my employer. I told myself I had moved on. I built a career, a family. I became "strong." Independent. Capable. But deep in that trauma, I made an unconscious vow: **"If I can stay in control… I can stay safe."**

And here's the irony: I had been groomed—then I learned to groom. To control. To manage. To mold others around me into what felt safe. The very behavior that hurt me became the strategy I used to protect myself.
I didn't realize it was fear driving the execution. Fear of being hurt again. Of being taken from. Of being powerless.

But grooming isn't leadership.
Control isn't peace.

And that's why I created **The Embodied Path** — not just a program, but a living, breathing map.
Not just mindset shifts, but nervous system resets. It's the seed. The nurture. The fruit. A full-body reclamation of trust and safety.

It's not for the faint of heart.
It's for the woman who's tired of surviving her own life.
Who's ready to feel again.
Who's ready to trust again.
Starting with herself.

If you're reading this, and some part of you is still holding it all together for everyone else — I see you.
If softness in your body feels foreign…
If your success has cost you your peace…
If you've mistaken control for power…

Perhaps you've also been grooming others to keep yourself safe.

Perhaps you've started to hear the loud silence too.

Let me tell you something:

You are not failing.
You are just tired.
And you don't have to carry it all anymore.
You are allowed to trust.
You are allowed to receive.
You are allowed to lead without bracing for impact.
And most of all?
You are allowed to choose a new way.
If this story resonated… maybe it's not just a story.

Maybe it's a sign.

Please know you're not too far gone. You're not broken. And you were never meant to do this alone. If the silence in your life has been feeling louder than ever, maybe real safety is on the other side of listening to the loud silence.

Heather Jones, CEO of The Next Chapter Endeavours, is a transformational coach, mentor, and leader who helps high-achieving women break free from cycles of mental overload and step into alignment, trust, and reclamation. Her mission is simple yet profound: to help women stop surviving and finally start living.

engage2elevate.ca

THE LIE BEHIND MOST
MARRIAGE FAILURES

NANCY LANDRUM

I grew up believing a comforting myth: **If you have love and commitment, your marriage will last.**

It sounds beautiful. It's also a lie.

I learned that the hard way.

Jim and I loved each other deeply. We were committed. Yet, day by day, our marriage was being eroded by one stubborn conflict we couldn't seem to solve.

My frustration came out as sarcastic put-downs and yelling. If Jim didn't understand me the first time, I simply said it louder. He finally began saying, "The louder you yell, the less I can hear you." He was right—sarcasm and shouting weren't helping me be heard.

Jim had his own go-to style: *You should have . . . Why didn't you . . .* accusations that only fueled my defensiveness.

We were locked in the age-old battle of *I'm right, you're wrong* — and we were losing ground every day.

How We Got Here

At twenty-three, I was widowed with two baby boys, ages two and eight months. Thirteen years later, I met Jim—also a widower with three children. It wasn't love at first sight, but he was fun, and I hadn't had much fun in my life. Loving him came easily. I said "yes," and we began planning our wedding.

We were both in our early forties—adults, seasoned by loss, confident that our love and maturity would carry us through.

But the day we returned from our honeymoon, we had a minor disagreement about a typical stepfamily issue. Over time, that "minor" issue grew into daily arguments. We were miserable, and love and commitment weren't enough to save us.

The Turning Point

It took excruciating pain for us to admit we needed help. The coach we found gave us two skills that changed everything:

1. Respectful Communication

No more sarcastic put-downs, yelling, or "you" accusations. Instead, we learned to speak from our own point of view: *When this happens, I feel . . . I'm concerned about . . . I would like . . .*

The first time we discussed our "hot issue" this way, we lasted forty minutes without a fight. It felt awkward, like speaking a foreign language, but when Jim opened his arms and said, "That felt so respectful. Let's try to always treat each other with respect," I agreed. From that moment, our goal shifted from winning arguments to protecting respect—24/7.

2. Anger Management

We also needed a way to cool down before talking. For me, that meant taking a thirty-minute "time out" to journal my anger until I calmed down. For Jim, it meant driving to a park, venting into a mini tape recorder, then erasing it before coming home.

The Third Leg of the Stool

Love and commitment are two legs of a marriage. The third is **respect**—supported by skills for communication and conflict management. Without respect, the stool tips over.

Once we had the skills, we never had another fight. Every few days, we took turns sharing our thoughts using our new methods. The respect made it easier to listen, understand, and feel empathy. Within weeks, we agreed on a solution to our "unsolvable" problem—and it worked.

From Struggle to Sharing

A few years later, Jim suggested we teach other couples what we had learned. We spent eleven years leading classes, speaking at marriage events, and writing our first book together, *How to Stay Married & Love It: Solving the Puzzle of a SoulMate Marriage.* I earned my master's in spiritual psychology, and we had plans to keep teaching for years.

Then Jim was diagnosed with terminal cancer. We had one precious year before he passed.

Why I Share This

I know some divorces are necessary. But over the past thirty years, I've watched hundreds of couples transform their marriages simply by learning and practicing respect.

Respect is the fertilizer that nourishes love and makes lifetime commitment a joy.

That's why I believe every couple—especially before marriage—should have access to classes that teach respectful communication and conflict resolution. Most of us only know the patterns we saw growing up, but there are better ways to share feelings, concerns, and desires that lead to the outcome we all want: to be heard, understood, and loved.

My mission is to reduce unnecessary divorces by exposing the myth that love and commitment are all you need.

If you want your love to last, make respect your third leg of the stool—and learn the skills to keep it strong.

Nancy Landrum has authored How to Stay Married & Love It, her first of eight books. The creator of an online relationship happiness course, Nancy has been featured in Yahoo, MSN, *The Washington Post*, and *Woman's Day*. Nancy helps couples learn to talk about anything without fighting, rediscover deep connection, and experience peace and lasting love.

millionairemarriageclub.com

FROM ASHES TO INFLUENCE: MY HEART-LED AWAKENING™ TO LEADERSHIP POWER

DEBI LYNN

"*Y*ou *are not broken—you are buried. And buried things are not dead. They are seeds.*"

The day I buried my son, Robert, was the day the world shifted under my feet.

He was only four months old—tiny, perfect, and gone far too soon.

Three days later, my boss called me into his office. My chair was still warm from the hours I had spent trying to hold myself together at work, pretending to function through the fog of grief. They told me my position had been "eliminated."

In one breath, I lost my child, my income, and my identity.

Grief had already stolen my sleep, my appetite, my energy, and my hope. Losing my job felt like the final blow—proof that the world was cold, unfair, and merciless. Yet I didn't realize the most dangerous loss was still ahead: losing myself.

The Weight of Invisible Disruptions

We often think of disruption as something external: an unexpected layoff, a diagnosis, a relationship ending. But the deeper disruption happens inside us. It's the quiet crumbling of self-worth. The erosion of confidence. The whisper in your mind saying, *This is it. You're done.*

In my case, grief didn't come alone. It brought financial strain, emotional exhaustion, and an aching loneliness that no one seemed to notice. I kept smiling for others, showing up, and pretending to be okay because the world rewards performance, not honesty.

People told me to "be strong." But strength, without a place to put the pain, can feel like a prison. And I was living in one.

The Breaking Point

There was a morning one month after Robert's funeral when I sat on the edge of my bed, staring at the wall. I had no job, no money coming in, and no plans. My phone buzzed with a past-due notice. The refrigerator held only condiments and a half-empty carton of milk. And my reflection in the mirror? I didn't recognize her.

I was breathing but not living.

That morning, a thought hit me hard: *If I don't change something, this is where I will stay.*

It wasn't a lightning bolt of motivation or a "rah-rah" moment. Instead, it was a quiet, gut-deep knowing. I could either keep letting life happen to me, or I could decide to happen to life.

The Rise: Finding the First Ember

I didn't start with a grand plan. I started with one question: "What is still mine?"

The answer was small but powerful:

- My voice
- My ability to learn
- My choice to keep going

Those became my lifelines.

I began reading everything I could about resilience, leadership, and human behavior. I attended workshops I could barely afford.

I reached out to women who inspired me, even when my voice trembled.

I remember sitting in the back row of a leadership seminar, feeling completely out of place. I didn't have a business yet. I didn't have a title to put on a name badge. But I took notes as if my life depended on it . . . because in a way, it did.

Slowly, I realized something: The very pain that had broken me was also giving me a lens of empathy, clarity, and grit that no textbook could teach.

Grief sharpened my vision for what mattered. Losing my job forced me to build something that couldn't be taken away. Nearly losing myself made me fiercely protective of my time, my energy, and my mission.

The Heart-Led Awakening™

My transformation wasn't overnight; it was a process of reclaiming my power in layers. Over time, I developed what I now call The Business CPR™ Method:

Passion—Reconnecting to what lights you up so you stop living on autopilot. This isn't just about hobbies or inspiration; it's about remembering the *why* behind your work, so you have fuel for the days when motivation fades.

Power—Owning your voice, your boundaries, and your value so you can lead with confidence. This means having the courage to say "no" without apology and "yes" without fear.

Profit—Building income in a way that feels aligned, sustainable, and soul-honoring without hustling for approval. This is where strategy meets soul, creating a business that supports your life, not swallows it.

I stopped asking, *Why me?* and started asking, *What now?*
I stopped measuring my worth by my paycheck and started measuring it by my impact.
I stopped seeing my story as a scar and started seeing it as my signature.

Turning Setbacks into Strategy

When you've been through deep loss, you carry two things that make you a force in leadership:

1. **A radar for what's real.** You no longer have patience for shallow, performative leadership—you speak to what matters.
2. **A resilience blueprint.** You've rebuilt from the ground up, so you know how to guide others when their foundation feels like it's cracking.

One of my clients came to me after losing a major business contract that had been her lifeline. She was terrified she'd have to close her doors. Using The Business CPR™ Method, we rebuilt her offers to align with her passion and created a simple but powerful marketing plan. Within six months, she had tripled her client base.

Another client, a high-achieving executive, was burnt out to the point of illness. She learned to set boundaries, delegate without guilt, and reconnect to her purpose. Within a year, she was leading her team with renewed energy and loving her work again.

I realized my pain had trained me to lead in a way that most people never experience. I could sit across from someone in their own storm and not flinch. I could help them see possibility when all they could see was rubble.

Why Your Disruption Can Be Your Divine Direction

Your disruption—whether it's loss, betrayal, burnout, or failure—isn't just a detour. It's an invitation.

It's a chance to:

- Discover what you're truly capable of when the safety nets are gone
- Strip away everything that's not aligned with your purpose
- Build something that can weather storms because it's rooted in who you are, not just what you do

When I embraced this, I stopped seeing my story as something to hide and started using it as a bridge. People don't follow perfection, they follow truth. And your truth, no matter how messy, can be powerful.

Leading with Heart in a World Obsessed with Hustle

Today, I guide women entrepreneurs and leaders to reclaim their energy, rebuild their confidence, and turn setbacks into sustainable success.

I've watched women who felt invisible step onto stages and own their voice. I've seen entrepreneurs on the verge of quitting turn passion into six-figure revenue streams. I've seen burned-out leaders rediscover why they started and lead with joy again.

It's not about pushing harder or working longer—it's about aligning business with heart. Because *profit without passion isn't success, it's just survival with a prettier view.*

You are not broken. You are buried.

And buried things are not dead; they are seeds. If you water those seeds with intention, protect them from the weeds of fear, and give them the light of aligned action, they will grow into something stronger than you can imagine.

The ashes you're standing in can become the fertile soil of your next chapter.

If my story resonates, it's because somewhere in your own journey, you've been carrying ashes of your own. Maybe it's the loss of a loved one, the collapse of a dream, the unraveling of a business, or the slow erosion of your energy and purpose.

Don't just survive this season. Lead yourself through it.

Start by asking yourself three questions:

1. What is still mine?
2. Where can I reclaim my voice today?

3. What small action can I take to prove to myself I am not done?

Write your answers. Then, take one step—no matter how small toward the vision you have for your life and business.

Here's a simple roadmap you can begin today:

Week 1 – Clarity: Identify your nonnegotiables in life and business. Journal about what drains you and what fuels you.

Week 2 – Boundaries: Remove one thing from your calendar that doesn't align with your goals.

Week 3 – Courage: Say "yes" to one opportunity that excites you, even if it scares you.

Week 4 – Creation: Take one step toward a dream project, product, or pivot, no matter how small.

By the end of thirty days, you'll see proof that you are moving, building, and leading.

If you're ready to stop carrying your disruption as a weight and start using it as your weapon, I'd love to walk with you.

Because you weren't meant to just get through this. You were meant to rise.

Debi Lynn is a business resilience strategist and certified grief educator who helps powerhouse women rise from disruption to domination through her Heart-Led Awakening™ programs. With a bold, heart-centered approach, Debi equips women to reclaim their energy, rebuild confidence, and create thriving businesses that honor their purpose.

heartledawakening.com

HEALTH BEGINS WITHIN

LYN MCCRIGHT AND
TERESA WALDING

I was a nurse who couldn't sit, stand, or even lie down without pain. Every muscle in my body ached. My lower back spasmed when I tried to rest, and I had to brace myself just to move from one chair to another. On the outside, I was the picture of professionalism—decades of experience, caring for patients with calm authority. On the inside, I was crumbling.

Like so many nurses, I had given everything to others and left almost nothing for myself. I had been trained to put patients first, to push through long shifts, to keep going no matter how drained I felt. But what I didn't realize was that in giving endlessly, I was slowly losing myself.

I tried everything. Medications, physical therapy, massage, acupuncture, even experimental treatments. Some gave temporary relief, but nothing touched the deeper misery. My pain wasn't just physical—it was emotional, spiritual. It wore me down, day by day, until I began to wonder if this was simply what my life would be now.

I was a nurse. I was supposed to be strong. But I was quietly breaking.

Then, in 2015, I attended a holistic nursing conference in Texas. I didn't know it at the time, but that gathering would change the course of my life. I sat in a crowded room, tired and skeptical, when I heard a speaker named Dr. Keith Blevens say something that stopped me in my tracks:

"Our experience of life is created from the inside out. If we are thinking it, we are feeling it."

At first, it sounded simple. Too simple. But something about those words cut through my exhaustion. This wasn't just information. Those words carried a truth I could feel.

It was as if someone had opened a window in a room I hadn't realized was suffocating me. Suddenly, I saw that my pain wasn't only about my body—it was shaped by my thoughts, by the meanings I gave to every sensation, by the awareness through which I experienced it all. In that moment, a peace I hadn't felt in years washed through me.

My body didn't magically heal, but my relationship with my pain shifted. I realized I wasn't broken. I wasn't powerless. The well-being I had been chasing all those years wasn't out there—it had been within me all along.

That realization was the seed that grew into an entirely new way of living. It set me on the path of nurse coaching, where I began to teach not from techniques and strategies, but from a deeper understanding of human resilience. And it gave me back something I thought I had lost forever: hope.

Lyn's Story

Around the same time, another nurse—my soon-to-be colleague and co-founder, Lyn—was on her own journey of discovery.

For Lyn, the breakthrough began with something she couldn't quite explain: automatic writing. She vividly remembers the moment—words flowing onto the page in a vision that was both beautiful and daunting. It felt like being handed a glimpse of a life she was meant to live, though she couldn't yet see how.

Soon after, Lyn stepped into leadership with the American Holistic Nurses Association. She began organizing conferences that shifted conversations in healthcare, putting resilience and inner wisdom at the forefront. Long before nurse coaching was formally recognized as a specialty, she was already embodying its heart: guiding people back to their wholeness.

Her journey was different from mine, but at its core, it pointed to the same truth: health and healing come from within.

The Three Principles

The foundation of our work—what became Advancing Holistic Health—rests on what are called the Three Principles, first articulated by Sydney Banks:

- Mind – the universal intelligence that animates all of life. The wisdom that grows a seed into a tree, that heals a cut without our instruction, that beats our hearts without effort.
- Thought – the creative power that shapes our inner experience, moment by moment. Thoughts drift across the mind like clouds, coloring the entire sky of our reality.
- Consciousness – the awareness that brings thought to life. Without consciousness, thought would be invisible. With it, our thoughts take form and feel real.

Together, these principles form the invisible operating system of being human. They explain why two people can walk through the same experience and live entirely different realities. They explain how a single moment of clarity can dissolve years of struggle.

For nurses, this understanding is transformative. In the old paradigm, pain is simply a signal to manage, stress a problem to fix, burnout an inevitable outcome of caring too much. But when we see through this lens, pain is not only physical—it is shaped by thought and awareness. Stress is not a fixed reality—it is an experience that can shift as our understanding deepens. And burnout is not inevitable—it is a signal inviting us to reconnect with what is always present: our inner resilience.

A New Way Forward

Everywhere we look, nurses are stretched thin. The weight of long shifts, short staffing, and constant emotional labor has left many burned out and questioning their place in the profession. Too often, those who give the most end up with the least left for themselves.

The old way of addressing this has been to add more: more tasks, more self-care checklists, more training. But more doesn't always heal. What's needed isn't another program or another layer of effort. What's needed is a shift in understanding.

When nurses see for themselves that their resilience and clarity come from within—not from fixing circumstances but from how they meet them—something changes. They bring a presence to patients that no technique can match. They lead with calm even in chaos. They rediscover compassion for themselves.

And when patients glimpse the same truth, they begin to trust their own wisdom. They make choices that support their well-being not because someone told them to, but because they see what truly matters for themselves.

This is how change happens in healthcare. Not through piling on more tools, but through a deeper understanding of what has been true all along.

The Vision

Imagine what could happen if the largest and most trusted profession on earth—nursing—embraced this understanding.

Every nurse touches countless lives. Each moment of clarity becomes a light that ripples outward: into families, into communities, into healthcare systems that desperately need healing themselves.

This is our vision:

- To teach millions of nurses the art of insight-based coaching
- To help people everywhere discover that they are not broken, but whole
- To support health systems in moving beyond short-term fixes toward sustainable well-being

And it is already beginning. Nurses are stepping into new confidence. Patients are awakening to their wisdom. Communities are remembering their capacity to heal.

Your Invitation

This story doesn't belong only to us. It belongs to every nurse who has ever stayed past their shift to comfort a patient. To every caregiver who has whispered a prayer for strength in the middle of the night. To every human being who has longed for peace in the midst of chaos.

What you are seeking is not far away. Joy, peace, and healing are not distant goals. They are already within you—your birthright, waiting to be understood.

As nurses deepen their understanding of resilience, they carry that light into patient rooms, into families, into communities. As patients see their wholeness, they begin to live from freedom rather than fear. And as we uncover this truth together, we don't just reshape healthcare—we reshape the very way we live.

Because what we understand within becomes the foundation for what we create together.

Lyn McCright and Teresa Walding are internationally known thought leaders on the future of nursing globally. Together they co-founded Advancing Holistic Health to chart a new, holistic path in healthcare. Through coaching, education, and mentoring, they help nurses reduce stress, reconnect with inner wisdom, and lead with clarity.

nursecoaching.com

BEING VISIBLE: MY JOURNEY FROM HIDING TO HELPING OTHERS SHINE

JOSETTE MANDELA

My journey toward being visible didn't start with a bold decision or a sudden "aha" moment. It began quietly, almost invisibly, back in my twenties.

I grew up in a household where money was never discussed—at least not in front of the children. We were taught that children should be seen and not heard, and "seen" didn't mean center stage. It meant polite, quiet, and out of the way. The path for women seemed simple: marry Prince Charming or work in a helping profession like customer service or social work. That was just "what women did."

But even as a young woman, I knew I wanted more. I just didn't know what "more" looked like.

When I met my own version of Prince Charming, I thought I'd found it. We married, and for seven years, life felt like a fairy tale. But fairy tales have plot twists. Mine came after a business trip.

I returned home to find that Prince Charming had transformed into something far less charming—let's just say the toad stage had arrived, and it wasn't cute.

The truth was, I'd never been comfortable dealing with money. It stressed me out, so when my husband offered to "take care of the finances," I gladly said, "Thank you!" And just like that, I abdicated all responsibility for our financial life. I never looked at the bank statements. I didn't even glance at the credit card statements—some of which were in my name alone. I simply assumed he was paying the bills, and I went about my business.

That business trip became a turning point. Questions about my marriage led me to quietly visit a lawyer to explore my options. And that's when the full depth of the financial mess I was in came crashing down on me. As I gathered documents to show our assets and liabilities, I discovered that every single credit card in my name was maxed out—along with their interest rates. Payments hadn't been made in months.

Suddenly, I was not only facing a divorce but also a financial crisis I'd had no idea was brewing. My lawyer told me that, in my situation, the best way forward wasn't to try to pay down the mountain of debt but to declare bankruptcy and start with a clean slate. I was young, naïve, and emotionally drained. I didn't really understand the long-term consequences, so I said yes.

About eighteen months after that fateful business trip, I was both divorced and bankrupt.

That's when the other shoe dropped. Bankruptcy came with its own set of challenges. Renting an apartment or turning on utilities required extra deposits, because companies wanted assurance I could pay them. Anytime I applied for something—an apartment, a service, even certain jobs—I could feel people silently wondering: *Is she going to do this to us too? Will we get paid?*

It was one of the most depressing times in my life. I'd gone from a single-family home to a small apartment. I was struggling to make ends meet, feeling like everything I'd worked for had evaporated. And worse, I had nothing to show for all my hard work.

I let myself have a pity party—for about six months. Then I decided something had to change. I couldn't keep living like this. I also realized I couldn't do it alone. I needed guidance. There was a missing piece in my understanding of money and wealth.

I looked around and saw women who appeared to "have it all." Some didn't even have jobs that paid as well as mine, yet they seemed financially secure. What did they know that I didn't? This was before the days of Google, YouTube tutorials, and online financial coaches. If you wanted answers, you had to find and ask people in the real world.

I started with my bank. I scheduled a meeting with the loan officer I'd worked with before and explained my situation. To my relief, he didn't judge me; instead, he educated me. He explained how I could take steps to rebuild my financial reputation and prove I was a good credit risk. He told me that the bankruptcy would stay on my record for ten years, and until then, I'd have to be proactive about showing lenders I was responsible.

One of his best suggestions was to get a secured credit card. At the time, I had about five hundred dollars in savings. He recommended using four hundred of that as collateral for a secured card. It worked like this: I could make purchases up to my limit, but when the bill came, I had to pay it—otherwise, the bank would pull the money directly from my savings account. If they had to do that, it would be another black mark against me.

I took his advice seriously. I used the card for small purchases, paid it in full every month, and guarded that account like a hawk. After a couple of years, the bank rewarded my consistency by upgrading me to an unsecured credit card. My limit was just five hundred dollars at first, but that small step felt like a huge win.

With each small win, my confidence grew. I started to think differently about money—not as a source of fear, but as something I could manage and control. That shift opened doors. I began building an emergency fund, contributing to a retirement account, and exploring ways to grow my wealth.

The next turning point happened by accident. I was at the mechanic's shop waiting for my car—six hours of waiting, to be exact. I'd come prepared with snacks and a notebook. And somewhere between snack breaks, a book poured out of me.

It wasn't planned. I didn't sit down and think, *I'm going to write a book.* But as I started jotting down thoughts about money—how to manage it, what I'd learned, the mistakes I'd made, and the questions I wished I'd asked—something clicked. If I'd struggled with money despite having a good job, I knew other women must be struggling too.

By the end of that long wait, I had the bones of a basic finance book.

But then I hit a wall. This was before Amazon made self-publishing easy. The only route was traditional publishing, and I didn't know where to start—or even if my book was worth publishing. I convinced myself the information was too obvious, forgetting that it was only "obvious" because I'd lived through the hard lessons to learn it.

So I tucked the manuscript away. Years passed. Decades, even. Life went on. I built my career, learned more about money, and quietly helped friends and family when they asked.

Then one day, I pulled out that old draft and read it with fresh eyes. And I realized something: My story—the messy, imperfect, not-at-all-fairy-tale story—could help women avoid the pain and confusion I'd endured. I could be a guide, a resource, and a reminder that financial freedom is possible, even if you've hit rock bottom.

That's when I decided to step into the light.

Being visible didn't come naturally to me. I'd spent most of my life hiding—first as the "seen but not heard" child, then as the wife who handed over all financial responsibility, and then as the woman who felt too ashamed to share her story. But I came to understand that my visibility isn't about me. It's about the women who need to see what's possible.

The women I serve now are often where I once was: successful in their careers, but quietly overwhelmed by money. They're making good money but still feel like they're behind. They don't know who to trust, and they're afraid of making costly mistakes. They want to grow wealth for themselves and their families, but they feel stuck, unsure of where to start.

I know that woman because I *was* that woman.

And now I can show her that she can move from confusion and fear to clarity and confidence. That she can learn where her money is going, make it work for her, and grow it in ways that feel aligned with her values. That she can ask the right questions, find trusted advisors, and take control of her financial future.

Today, I'm not just managing my own money—I'm helping other women manage and grow theirs. I'm visible because my story might be the spark that lights someone else's path.

And if that means stepping out from behind the curtain and telling the world how I went from fairy-tale beginnings to financial disaster to freedom, then so be it. Because visibility isn't about perfection. It's about connection. And I'm here for every woman ready to take that first, imperfect, but powerful step toward her own freedom.

Josette Mandela is a financial power-house and resilience expert dedicated to empowering women to take charge of their financial futures. A bestselling author, Josette provides practical, accessible strategies for wealth-building and personal growth. Her mission is to help women gain confidence, achieve financial independence, and embrace the abundant lives they deserve.

josettemandela.com

THE ENTREPRENEUR'S GUIDE TO BUILDING YOUR DREAM TEAM: *HOW THE BEST TEAMS PUT YOUR BUSINESS IN THE SPOTLIGHT*

JESSPER MAQUINDANG

Several months ago, I was speaking to an entrepreneur who was looking for ways to expand her presence on social media. Let's call her Annelisse. My conversations with Annelisse are typically pleasant, but this particular day she was feeling down. I asked, "Annelisse, what's going on?" She revealed that she had a team member who was not putting the right amount of effort into his role. Let's call him Winslow.

Annelisse had hired Winslow to respond to comments and post new content daily on social media. Simple enough, right? Unfortunately, no. Was he responding to comments? Yes. Was he posting new content daily? Yes. But how often? Not much. The minimum— just enough to say the job was done, but not enough to build real traction. As a result, the outcome was less than stellar. When Annelisse met with Winslow to discuss his performance, there was a constant back-and-forth: He would say the job was done. She would say it wasn't enough . . . and on and on. During my conversation with Annelisse, she told me how upset she felt. "The tasks and responsibilities for this job are just *common sense*," she remarked.

Common sense? We'll get back to this.

I realized that this is not an uncommon situation. As a Senior Professional in Human Resources (SPHR), I've seen similar instances where business owners and team members were not on the same page. An entrepreneur may feel that a certain team member is not keeping pace. In many cases, it was a lack of clear expectations or a lack of clear decision-making processes.

Annelisse was convinced her situation was common sense. But what might be common sense to one person may not be common sense to someone else. What was the volume and frequency of comments and posts that were expected of Winslow? When, where, why, what, how? Winslow never knew.

Fortunately, Annelisse understood she had to take the time to pull Winslow aside and have a meaningful conversation about setting new expectations and discussing what they could do together to make real progress. Now, with clear expectations in place, Winslow had a better idea about what success in his role looked like.

When entrepreneurs and business owners have the right pieces in place to help their employees, virtual assistants, and contractors succeed, it sets the foundation for a Dream Team. Let's build that Dream Team for you. Let's build something that will put your business in the spotlight.

The Hidden Costs of an Ineffective Team

Before we look at building a Dream Team, let's consider the costs of having an ineffective team. What happens if you don't take the time to put the right pieces in place? To begin with, your business can suffer from lower productivity because an ineffective team can cause delays in getting work done on time, leading to missed deadlines. Second, your business can lose revenue because having an ineffective team can lead to poor customer service, resulting in lost sales. Third, your business can struggle with higher operating costs because team inefficiencies can require more tools, more software, and more resources to keep everyone on the same page.

As a result, you spend a lot of time fixing mistakes. You end up getting stuck in the small details instead of focusing on the big vision and larger strategy. Your business can miss out on visibility opportunities as well. Yes, you could have been spending more time sharing your impact with the world, but you were too distracted from constantly putting out fires. There were missed opportunities to build your brand, scale your business, and connect with the people who need your message most. But there is a solution: you guessed it—building your Dream Team!

The D.R.E.A.M. Team Framework

Where do we start? I created a process I call the The D.R.E.A.M. Team Framework. Within this team-building process, D.R.E.A.M. serves as an acronym.

Define the vision and values. As you're building your Dream Team, you want your employees, virtual assistants, and contractors to see the big picture of what you're working toward. *What does your business stand for? Who do you serve? Why do you serve?* These are very important questions to answer, and you want to be able to share that with your team.

Recruit with intention. When you're looking for new team members, you want to make sure that they're a culture fit, not just a fit for the task. When it comes to culture fit, you want to make sure new team members align with the values, vision, and mission of your business. When your people are aligned, they'll feel more engaged and more motivated to go above and beyond. Your team members become more productive because they believe in what you value in your business.

Establish clarity. In clear terms, what does success look like? When people make mistakes, how can they fix things? Show clarity in roles and responsibilities, the processes, the structures, what your business is working toward. That way, your employees will get a clear picture of what they need to do to complete their tasks successfully.

Activate accountability. Give your team members more ownership in the decision-making process. Give them opportunities to develop their own solutions to the problems and challenges in your business. When you give your team members more ownership, you send a powerful message: "Your voice matters. Your insights are valuable." This creates a sense of empowerment for your employees. People naturally step up when they feel trusted. They think more critically. They take initiative. They care more deeply about the results because they've played a role in shaping the path forward.

Multiply impact. Keep an eye out for what's working... and do more of that. Too often, entrepreneurs shift focus too quickly, chasing the next problem or opportunity. But high-performance teams grow faster and more sustainably when they amplify what already delivers results. It's not just about doing more. It's about doing more of what matters. Multiply what's already creating impact for your team and watch how that momentum lifts your entire business.

When you put all the elements of the D.R.E.A.M. Team Framework into practice, you create more than just a team—you create a culture of trust, clarity, and shared purpose. Each step builds on the last, ensuring your people feel connected to the vision, confident in their roles, and empowered to contribute their best work. This is how you transform a group of individuals into a high-performing Dream Team, one that not only meets goals but exceeds them, driving sustainable growth and long-term success for your business.

Why Your Business Needs an HR Strategy

Far too many small business owners assume that HR is something only large corporations need to worry about. Human Resources is an important area in any business that involves people. Without an HR strategy, you're more likely to hire reactively, experience burnout, deal with costly turnover, or get caught in legal or compliance issues. Without an HR strategy, you'll keep putting out fires instead of focusing on the future. Without an HR strategy, your impact is limited by how much you can handle alone.

With the right HR foundation, you can more effectively build your Dream Team, reduce burnout and turnover, and free up more time to focus on growth. Human Resources is more than just administrative tasks; HR is a powerful accelerator for building a business that's resilient, profitable, and ready for the spotlight.

Elevate Your Team, Elevate Your Visibility

There's a famous African proverb: "If you want to go fast, go alone. But if you want to go far, go together." As an entrepreneur, you're serving others. You have a message to share with the world. It's difficult to spread your message when you're doing everything by yourself. But when you have the right people by your side, your impact multiplies.

Don't fall into the same trap as Annelisse did. Avoid costly hiring mistakes. Avoid losing time from constantly fighting fires. Avoid the emotional toll it can have on you. Find people who align with your vision. When you have a Dream Team that puts your business in the spotlight, you gain more visibility in the world. An effective team reduces your involvement in day-to-day tasks, allowing you to focus on speaking on more stages, creating thought leadership content, and building partnerships and media relationships. That's right—building a Dream Team will help you stand out in the marketplace.

Jessper Maquindang, a certified Senior Professional in Human Resources (SPHR), helps entrepreneurs build high-performing teams. He equips founders with systems and strategies that strengthen every stage of the employment cycle. A passionate marathon runner, Jessper believes sustainable growth in business and life comes from embracing purpose, resilience, and optimism.

famileadconsulting.com

SHOW ME THE MONEY! (AND FIND ME MORE TIME TOO!)

LEE MUNCH

Visibility comes in many forms. I am here to make the money in your bank account more visible, as well as your family more visible because you have more time to spend with them, without the nagging worry of your business.

Heart-centered entrepreneurs and business owners tell me the number-one they need more of is more business. They are working so hard, doing really great things, doing all the right things, and yet there doesn't seem to be more money in their actual bank account, they are tired, and they don't understand why. Not a day goes by when I don't hear a business owner saying same thing and feeling frustrated, overwhelmed, and at a loss of what to do.

This might even be you.

The first thing I want to tell you is that you're not alone. There is a way out, and it doesn't even necessarily require you getting more business. Because the truth of the matter is more business always means more work, and if you are already overworked and over-stressed as a result, you're only going to exacerbate the situation. In fact, when people tell me they need more business, what they really mean is they want *more money*.

So, if you would like more money AND more time without more business, then keep reading! I call myself a business "alchemist" because I find the things that are not working (the lead) and "magically" (not really) turn them in to seamless, consistently growing GOLD. This is how I got my nickname, the Business "Gold Digger," because I love going on treasure hunts in businesses to dig up the currently hidden money and time. And that's how I can "show you the money"—right in your pocket and bank account.

Money and time are the flip sides of the same coin. We invest time to get more money, and we invest money to get more time. Notice I use the word *invest*. This is where we begin, as the desired outcome is to have more of both. Unfortunately, most of us (yes, even me at times) SPEND our money and our time—in other words, once they're gone, they're gone, and we have less of both.

Right now, by reading this chapter, you are investing a little time so you can have more of it and more money. There are so many places that money and time "hide," and when you find one, you'll feel like you won the lottery. Because once you know, you cannot ever unknow again. And the best part? You have just turned that "lead" in your business in to solid gold, which works in all economic, political, and crazy world event environments!

Here are three common places money and time are waiting to be dug up to give you instant money in your pocket and/or more time in your day:

1. **Haphazard Enrollment Flow (aka Sales Process)**

   The enrollment flow in my opinion has three objectives: build a relationship, provide value, and be of service—regardless of the outcome. When properly designed and implemented, you serve all at different levels and enroll those who are a good fit. I see over and over again business owners who give so much to any and all, which means they are spending too much time on the wrong people, and not enough on the right people.

From the time someone learns about you until they throw their credit card at you, things happen. Regardless of how fast or slow the process is, it is pretty much the same for every new client. I find many times we are so anxious to help our potential clients and "save the world" that we don't take the time to determine if they are a good fit or seriously interested in our assistance. So we end up spending a lot of time, energy, and even money that would be better invested elsewhere.

Let's Fix That

What are the steps in your process? You have them; you just may not really use them as effectively as possible. To "dig them up," go through a recent or current interaction to determine the actual steps. When your enrollment flow is documented, it becomes a deselection process where only those who are serious and a right fit get to the end 80 percent of the time. When your enrollment flow is documented, you can easily turn up the client "flow" in growth mode and turn it down when in integration. This allows for seamless consistency that works all the time.

2. Entrepreneurial ADD (aka Bright Shiny Object Syndrome)

Let's face it, most of us have this to a certain degree. I myself used to suffer from it. Then I discovered the prescription for it (there's no cure that I have found as of yet).

It is so easy to get caught up in just about anything until something else takes our attention. For instance, you are creating some content when the phone rings. You answer it; you get involved in a conversation; you hang up. You return to your work and realize you forgot where you were.

Think of it this way. The person contacting you knows why they are there. You may or may not know who they are or why they are contacting you. Plus, as you were involved in something else, when you respond to them, there's a slight disconnect. The person starts talking and explaining. You need a moment or so to catch on. Then you have a conversation that can go on for who knows how long. Once completed, there's another moment or so of disconnect. You then return to your work and now need to remember where you were and what you were in the middle of doing before the interruption, so you need to backtrack. I have spent many hours lost this way when working with folks.

Let's Fix That

Create a time of day when people can access you (like office hours). Another option is using Marco Polo for communication. However, to make it the most beneficial and most efficient, before someone gets in touch with you during this time, they must text or email what they want to discuss. This way you are prepared and can respond and resolve things quicker.

3. **It's Not about the Money**

Many heart-centered entrepreneurs often say, "It's not about the money." Here's the thing, though. It's not about the money; it's about the results your clients get. However, unless you have a genie in a bottle or the universe is paying your bills, it *is* about the money. Money is how we transact. When we are struggling, we are stressed and cannot truly be our best. When we have more than enough, we can help so many more people! It makes making a real impact much easier. Remember, money and time are the flip side of the same gold coin. The difference is that money can come, go, and come again.

Time, while we are here on Planet Earth, is finite. We all get the same twenty-four hours a day. This means at some point we can only give so much of our time.

Knowing and understanding five simple numbers in our business will make all the difference in the world. Every business. Every industry. Once you know them, you know them. And once you use them, you have control in your business, regardless of what is happening. Tracking can be easy. In fact, when you know them, just by improving each of them by as little as 15 percent, you most likely will double your profit.

Let's Fix That

The five areas to start tracking are:

- Leads (marketing): how many people interact with you (every industry is different)
- Conversion rate (sales): how many of the leads become clients
- Average dollar sale: how much each client invests with you on average
- Number of transactions: how often they buy from you
- Profit: time, money, and income

So now we have three ways to make your money more visible in the bank and time more visible by more life. You can now start digging for the hidden gold that brings relief and control. Once you know the five ways, you can learn strategies to improve them, so you don't just find gold—you create it.

You want to make a difference. Your future clients need you to make that difference for them! So what are you waiting for? If not you, who? If not now, when?

Lee Munch has always been about making money. For the past nineteen years, combining analytics, heart, and soul, Lee's 5-ways methodology and her results-driven Business Alchemy Programs ensure entrepreneurs simplify, grow, and thrive consistently. Lee has been featured on *Oprah & Friends* and shared the stage with T. Harv Eker.

businessblissacademy.com

operations. My family learned that growth often complicated their ability to rely solely on family labor.

The Harsh Realities: When Things Go Wrong

The most sobering questions emerged as the business matured:

- What happens if someone becomes unable to work?
- Will the business survive if someone is injured or dies?
- What about key family members or employees you depend on daily?

I witnessed devastating consequences when families failed to address these questions. Some relatives trusted spouses completely, sharing financial dreams and business goals, only to watch those dreams shatter when partners prioritized personal needs over collective family futures. The results included separation, divorce, and financial ruin. Recovery from such betrayals typically requires five years or more, similar to recovering from major life disruptions.

My Professional Journey: From Healthcare to Financial Services

As a Licensed Respiratory Care Practitioner, I managed pulmonary rehabilitation, adult fitness, and sleep disorder programs. I helped patients with chronic lung disease, heart conditions, and cancer learn to live better despite health challenges. Daily, I heard stories of people choosing between food and medication, or moving back with ex-spouses because they couldn't afford independent living and feared running out of money.

The medical field began prioritizing technology over patient care. Documentation systems shifted focus from patients to productivity metrics. Consultants who never interacted with patients determined how many clients staff could see daily. The system emphasized efficiency over effectiveness, metrics over human connection.

I realized many health problems connected directly to financial stress. Patients couldn't afford proper nutrition, medication, or basic healthcare. Their financial illiteracy was making them physically sicker.

This revelation drove my career transition. I needed education and resources to help middle-class families, women, business owners, entrepreneurs, and working-class individuals being exploited by profit-driven industries. It was time to provide honest financial guidance, helping people expand their financial futures while protecting their hopes, dreams, and goals. Running out of money should never keep anyone awake at night.

The Money Truth: Making Your Dollars Work Harder

Money doesn't grow on trees, but it can grow beyond what typical financial providers offer. Many companies require large minimum investments while overlooking middle-class families, women, and business owners seeking help to build wealth while protecting their financial journey from excessive taxes, fees, low interest rates, and administrative costs.

Like most people, I wondered how to keep more of my hard-earned money and reduce financial losses. As a financial professional, I found answers. Lifestyles, behaviors, mindset, and attitudes combined with financial knowledge impact far more than individual bank accounts. Every financial choice improves, depletes, or devastates circumstances for the short-term, long-term, or lifetime.

Life isn't always fair. Biblical wisdom teaches that hardships reveal strength we didn't know we possessed, strength we can share with others facing similar challenges. Whether circumstances feel fair or unfair, we choose our response.

I found myself in a JOB (Just Over Broke) situation like many people. These circumstances led me to seek better understanding and solutions for myself and others facing similar financial challenges.

My Mission: Ending Financial Illiteracy

- Financial illiteracy represents an economic crisis affecting more than 5 billion people worldwide. Limited by financial struggles, inflation, rising living costs, and lack of financial education, these barriers impact lifetime wealth building. Less than 10 percent of Americans live in a household with a net worth exceeding one million dollars.

I'm on a mission to eliminate financial illiteracy. I'm disrupting industries that exploit the middle class, women, business owners, and hardworking families by restricting access to financial education and wealth building tools that wealthy families use routinely.

Wealthy individuals understand how to minimize taxes, fees, penalties, and administrative costs. They've learned to navigate and manage their money with professional help to grow and protect wealth with less stress. They understand that financial freedom means always generating more income opportunities. This knowledge shouldn't remain exclusive to the privileged few.

My grandpa understood these principles. He planned one hundred years of wealth-building starting at age eighteen. This generational thinking separates those who build lasting wealth from those who work hard but struggle financially.

Are you ready for change? Do you want to learn more about your financial journey?

Wouldn't it be freeing to know the amount of money you need to support your lifestyle, dreams, and goals while pursuing your American Dream? It's possible! You don't know what you don't know until someone shows you how financial resources and strategies can transform your future

Key Takeaways for Your Financial Success:

- Strategic thinking trumps hard work alone. Calculate risks and diversify like successful farmers do.

- Plan for business protection and succession. Don't let unfore-seen events destroy your achievements.

- Financial literacy directly affects your health and the quality of your life. Money stress creates genuine health problems.

- Professional guidance prevents costly mistakes. Learn from proven expertise and experience.

- Generational wealth planning begins today. Think beyond your lifetime like my grandparents did.

Your Choice Shapes Your Legacy

Time, health, and age wait for no one. Each day offers new opportunities for you, your business, and your family. Will you align financially to build lasting wealth, or fade as years pass?

You deserve more time, money, and financial freedom to pursue your dreams. The roadmap to financial independence exists. Your choice matters—not just for you, but for generations of your family's future.

Bonnie Piel is a financial service educator and professional agent with How Money Works, and she is dedicated to stomping out financial illiteracy. Bonnie understands the challenges of building sustainable wealth, and her mission is disrupting industries and providing her clients with a roadmap to financial freedom and generational wealth-building.

howmoneyworks.com/bonniepiel

THE VISIBLE REBEL— BUILDING SPEAKER AUTHORITY THROUGH CHANNELED RAGE

HOLLIS PIRKEY

T he most powerful moment of my speaking career happened while I was having a colonoscopy.

Stay with me here—I know this isn't where you expected a chapter on speaker visibility to start, but that's exactly the point. Real visibility doesn't come from polished perfection. It comes from the raw, uncomfortable moments when your truth finally erupts through the carefully constructed facade of "professional success."

My phone buzzed as the doctor began the procedure. A client was having an "emergency"—their Facebook ad had been disapproved. Without thinking, I reached for my phone. The nurse looked horrified. The doctor said, "Sir, can you please put the phone down?" Through the sedation haze, I slurred, "Just one second; this is important."

His response changed everything: "So is your colon."

That moment of absolute absurdity—lying exposed in a hospital gown, prioritizing a client's minor inconvenience over my own health—became the cornerstone of my most requested keynote speech. It's the story that gets me booked for high-ticket speaking engagements and attracts my ideal clients: angry divorced C-suite executives and entrepreneurs who recognize their own imprisonment in that hospital room scene.

The Paradox of Invisible Success

Here's what twenty years of building businesses taught me: The more available you make yourself, the less visible you become. You transform into a utility, like electricity or running water—essential but unnoticed until something goes wrong. Your expertise becomes commoditized. Your boundaries evaporate. Your unique voice is drowned out in the constant stream of immediate responses and perpetual availability.

Most speakers believe visibility means being everywhere, all the time. They post on seventeen platforms, accept every podcast invitation, speak at every free networking event, and answer every email within minutes. They mistake motion for momentum, presence for power. They become professionally invisible—everywhere and nowhere simultaneously.

The divorced executives in my audience know this exhaustion intimately. They built empires while their marriages crumbled. They achieved everything except what really mattered. Their anger isn't just about business; it's about the systematic betrayal of their own values in pursuit of a success that ultimately feels hollow. When I share my colonoscopy story from the stage, I watch recognition flash across their faces. They've all been there, metaphorically or literally, sacrificing their dignity for someone else's convenience.

Anger as Your Visibility GPS

Your rage isn't a liability—it's your most authentic differentiator. The speaking industry is drowning in motivational platitudes and recycled wisdom. What cuts through the noise isn't another framework or methodology. It's the speaker who dares to voice what everyone thinks but no one says.

The anger you feel about your industry's dysfunction? That's your keynote. The fury about outdated business models? That's your book. The rage about sacrificing everything for ungrateful clients? That's your signature story.

When I started speaking about my colonoscopy revelation, meeting planners initially hesitated. "Is that appropriate?" they asked. But audiences erupted. Finally, someone was telling the truth about entrepreneurial imprisonment. My speaking calendar exploded—not despite my anger-fueled message, but because of it.

Consider the most visible speakers in any industry. They're not the ones playing it safe. They're the rebels channeling productive rage into transformation. They're the ones who dare to say, "This is broken, and here's how we fix it." Your anger gives you permission to break ranks, to challenge conventions, to become the speaker everyone quotes at dinner.

The Orca Strategy for Sustainable Visibility

Usually, I'm a whitewater kayaker, but six months after my medical wake-up call, I was visiting Laguna Beach and decided to try paddleboarding. There, I encountered a pod of orcas. These eight-thousand-pound apex predators taught me more about sustainable visibility than any business book ever could.

Orcas don't hunt constantly. They work in pods, maintaining clear roles and boundaries. They surface when necessary, dive deep when needed, and never apologize for their power. They're simultaneously the ocean's most visible and most strategic predators.

This became my visibility model: Surface powerfully, deliver value intensely, then disappear completely. No constant social media presence. No perpetual availability. No diluted messaging across countless platforms. Instead, concentrated bursts of transformational content followed by deliberate absence.

I now speak at fewer events per year. Each appearance is crafted, powerful, and commands attention because scarcity creates value. Between events, I'm not invisible—but close to it, by design. No random podcast appearances. No free strategy sessions. No coffee meetings to "pick my brain."

The result? Event planners compete for my attendance. My speaking fee is increasing since I reduced my availability by 70 percent. The less accessible I became, the more visible my message grew.

Engineering Your Breakthrough Moment

Every speaker needs their "colonoscopy story"—that moment of brutal honesty that defines their message. But here's what most speakers get wrong: They manufacture these moments instead of mining them from their genuine rage.

Your breakthrough visibility moment already exists in your anger. What industry practice infuriates you? What accepted wisdom makes you want to scream? What "normal" business behavior reveals systemic dysfunction? That's your visibility goldmine.

For my divorced executive clients, their breakthrough often comes from the intersection of personal and professional collapse. The midnight email that ended their marriage. The missed recital that broke their child's heart. The hospital bed where they realized nobody from their company visited. These aren't just stories;

they're visibility weapons that cut through market noise with surgical precision.

Document your rage moments. The email that made you throw your phone. The client request that made you question everything. The industry event where you wanted to stand up and scream, "This is all bullshit!" These become your signature stories, your keynote frameworks, your book chapters.

The Boundary Revolution Creates Visibility

Counterintuitively, the stricter your boundaries, the more visible you become. When I announced I would only check email twice weekly, my inbox exploded with panic. When I declared Fridays through Mondays off-limits, clients predicted business suicide. When I tripled my speaking fees overnight, colleagues called me delusional.

Every boundary I set amplified my visibility. Why? Because in a world of perpetual availability, boundaries become rebellion. And rebellion gets noticed.

Here's my current visibility infrastructure:

- Speaking: Fewer events annually, led to higher rates per keynote
- Email: Checked Tuesdays and Thursdays, 48-hour response minimum
- Content: One monthly article that challenges industry norms
- Availability: Ten hours weekly, period
- Podcast appearances: Two annually, only on industry-leading shows

This isn't arrogance; it's architecture. Every "no" elevates the value of your "yes." Every boundary becomes a billboard for your expertise.

Every restriction reinforces your positioning as someone worth waiting for.

The Client Transformation Conversation

Visibility without conversion is just expensive vanity. The rage that fuels your message must transform into results for your audience. This requires a fundamental shift in how you position your speaking and expertise.

I now open every speaking inquiry with this: "I'm excellent at what I do. I'm also excellent at living my life. I speak at select events that align with my message of sustainable success through strategic boundaries. My fee reflects transformation, not just information. If you're looking for someone to fill a slot cheaply, I'm not your speaker. But if you want someone who will fundamentally shift how your audience thinks about success, let's talk."

Half immediately disappear. Perfect. The half who remain are ready for transformation, not just entertainment.

Measuring Visible Impact

Traditional speakers measure success through volume: speeches given, people reached, social media followers accumulated. Lifestyle speakers measure differently: Revenue per speech, not number of speeches. Transformation stories, not attendee counts. Quality of life maintained, not opportunities accepted. Message clarity, not market coverage.

My favorite metric? Days since I've compromised my values for visibility—currently at 847 and counting.

When you build visibility through channeled rage and maintained boundaries, you attract only those ready for real change. Your audience self-selects for transformation. Your message resonates with those who matter, repels those who don't.

Your Visibility Revolution Starts Now

Your speaker visibility journey doesn't require you to be everywhere. It requires you to be somewhere, powerfully, with a message that channels collective rage into productive transformation. The divorced executives and burnt-out entrepreneurs in your audience don't need another motivational speaker. They need someone who voices their fury and shows them how to transform it into a lifestyle that actually works.

The speaking industry tells you visibility requires constant hustle, perpetual presence, and unlimited accessibility. But look at the speakers who truly matter—the ones whose messages create movements. They're not the most available; they're the most authentic. They channel their anger into architecture, their rage into revenue, their boundaries into breakthrough visibility.

Your colonoscopy moment is waiting. Your orca wisdom is circling. Your rage is ready to become your most powerful visibility tool.

The question isn't whether you'll become visible. It's whether you'll become visible on your terms, with your boundaries intact, living a life that would make those orcas proud—powerful, strategic, and absolutely unwilling to sacrifice your well-being for someone else's definition of success.

The stage is waiting. But it's waiting on your schedule, at your price, with your message of transformation through channeled rage.

Welcome to visibility that actually works.

Hollis Pirkey is an award-winning writer, producer, and director with twenty-six years in the entertainment industry, plus a decade running an acclaimed landscape construction firm. Today, he helps others convert destructive anger into positive change, proving it's never too late to reclaim lasting personal peace and resilience.

angerchanneling.com

STEP INTO THE LIGHT: A SPEAKER'S JOURNEY TO BEING SEEN

JASE SOUDER

You have a message. Not a suggestion, not a nice idea—but a mission. And deep down, you know it's time to stop hiding and start speaking.

This chapter is for the speakers, coaches, and leaders who feel called—but stuck. You're not lacking talent. You're lacking visibility. And the longer you stay quiet, the heavier it feels—like your voice is fading while your mission waits.

But what if there were a path forward? What if there were three steps from the wings to the spotlight?

Before You Step into the Spotlight . . .

I want you to imagine you're backstage—just behind the curtain. You can hear the audience buzzing. You feel the lights warming the stage. You know you're supposed to be out there.

But before you take that final step into the spotlight, you notice something.

There are three spotlights shining down—right there in the wings. Each one lights up a different part of your path. And when you step into them, one by one, they prepare you for the main stage. They don't just light the way—they activate you.

Those spotlights are:

- Step into the Light
- Claim the Crown
- Shine Like You're Sent

Let's walk through each one together.

Step into the Light

For years, I lived in the wings—close enough to hear the applause but never stepping forward. I had a message in my heart, but fear gripped my throat. I told myself I wasn't ready, wasn't polished, wasn't enough.

One day, I watched someone on stage say something I had thought a thousand times—but they weren't shaking. They weren't hiding. And the audience leaned in like it was oxygen. That's when I realized: They weren't better than me. They were just willing to go first.

Stepping into the light isn't about ego. It's about obedience. It's saying, "I'll go," even if your knees shake and your voice cracks. It's choosing purpose over perfection.

If you've been lingering in the shadows—waiting for the perfect moment—it's time. Not when you're more polished, or more prepared. *Now.* Your message won't serve anyone locked inside your head. And someone out there is praying for the exact words only you can say.

You don't have to be famous to be effective. You just have to be visible. And visibility isn't vanity—it's responsibility. When you finally step into the light, you're not just doing it for you. You're doing it for the ones still hiding, the ones still hurting, the ones who don't believe their voice matters until they see you use yours.

So step in. Speak up. And shine.

Claim the Crown

There's a moment in every speaker's journey when they stop asking for permission—and start walking in authority.

For me, it came the day I realized I was diluting my voice to sound more "professional." I trimmed the edges off my truth. I softened my story. And what did I get? Polite applause and zero conversions.

Then someone pulled me aside and said, "I didn't connect with you because I couldn't feel you." That hit hard. Because it was true. I was still wearing the crown someone else handed me—instead of claiming the one I was born with.

To claim the crown means you stop performing and start aligning. You speak from soul, not script. You let your quirks and convictions show. You stop trying to impress—and start aiming to connect.

And if you're wondering if you're "qualified" to wear that crown? Let me remind you: God doesn't call the qualified. He qualifies the called.

When you claim the crown, everything starts to click. You're no longer mimicking your mentors—you're embodying your mission. Your presence gets bigger. Your message gets clearer. And your impact gets deeper.

You no longer shrink to fit the mold. You stretch to fit the mission.

So go ahead. Own your story. Own your edge. Own your anointing.

Your crown isn't up for vote. It's already yours. Put it on.

Shine Like You're Sent

Once you've stepped into the light and claimed your crown, there's one more move: shining like you were sent to the stage.

Because you were.

There's a difference between showing up—and showing up on assignment. When you know you're sent—not just by strategy but by Spirit—your delivery changes. You don't just speak; you transmit. People don't just hear you; they feel you.

Imagine this: You step on stage. Your heart is pounding. You're holding a powerful message you've crafted and rehearsed with care. And then—you breathe. You don't scramble. You don't perform. You speak from your gut—not because you're improvising, but because you've done the work ahead of time. You know your story. You trust your voice. You're ready.

And something shifts. Your posture settles. Your power lands. The room softens. And someone comes up after and says, "I don't know what just happened, but I think my life changed."

That's what happens when you shine like you're sent.

When you speak, people feel the difference. Your message doesn't just inform—it transforms. You become a mirror reflecting their possibility, a megaphone amplifying what they didn't even know they needed to hear.

This isn't hype. This is holy. You're not there to impress—you're there to ignite.

So when your moment comes—when the mic is in your hand and the lights are on—don't just deliver. Radiate. Speak with joy, with fire, with divine clarity.

Because it's not about being perfect.

It's about being placed.

Your Next Step

If you saw yourself in these pages—if something deep said, "Yes, this is me"—then know this:

You're not crazy for wanting more. You're not arrogant for wanting a stage. You're called. And that calling isn't going away.

You don't need to hustle harder or wait for "someday." You just need to take the next step into the light. And I'd be honored to guide you.

Your visibility is not a luxury—it's a lifeline. Your mission matters too much to stay silent. And your audience? They're already waiting.

The world is waiting for the sound only you can make. Let's make sure they hear it!

Jase Souder is a public speaker, bestselling author, and the founder of World Class Speaker Academy. He's been published in books with co-authors such as Deepak Chopra, Anthony Robbins, and Mark Victor Hansen and appeared on national TV and radio. Jase helps people create massive impact, raving fans, and a rush of new clients with every presentation.

jasesouder.com

VISIBILITY

DIANE STRAND

When I hear the word *visibility*, I think about being seen in a way that shines a spotlight on you and your brand, where your presence draws in like-minded people and clients. To me, visibility is a tool. It's not just about being noticed; it's about building credibility and giving people a glimpse into your expertise. It's about showing people your authority so they can trust you before they even meet you.

In today's world, visibility is one of the most powerful marketing tools you can have. It's essential. Without visibility, you can scream your message as loudly as you want, but no one will hear you.

I didn't always know the importance of visibility. Early in my entrepreneurship, I was less visible, and everything was harder. Finding clients, closing sales, and even having people understand what my business could offer them—these were all difficult tasks. Once I became more visible, my business grew faster, and the results were exponential. Momentum builds on itself: The more visible you are, the more visible you want to be, and the more visible you become. Leadership doesn't get easier; it just becomes more public. And if you want to make an impact, you must be seen and heard so people can connect with your message.

Visibility Is Both Claimed and Earned

I believe visibility is both something you *claim* and something you *earn*.

Claiming visibility means owning your voice, creating opportunities for yourself, and putting in the sweat equity. No one else is going to hand it to you; they're too busy building their own. You have to step forward and claim it.

Earning visibility comes as you move through levels of exposure. You don't just show up on *Good Morning America* out of nowhere. You start with small articles, podcasts, and local TV. As you build credibility and consistency, you move into larger media markets.

For me, it began with pitching small articles and podcasts. At first, I was chasing guest spots, but over time, media outlets began calling me. Today, I've been seen on ABC, interviewed on morning shows across major markets, featured on the NYSE stage, and even on the cover of *Female Entrepreneur.* Those moments didn't happen overnight; they were earned step-by-step.

Visibility takes your expertise and authority and turns it into credibility—and credibility brings more visibility. That credibility, combined with experience, is what makes people choose you over someone else who may have the same skills, but no public presence.

The Plateau—and the Shift

There was a point, right before COVID-19, when my business plateaued. It felt like I had hit a ceiling. That's when I realized I needed to change my approach to social media.

I started sharing my wins: awards, features, speaking engagements. I realized it wasn't bragging. It was letting people know what I was doing, so they could connect with it. Sharing accolades builds trust and credibility.

That shift brought me full circle to my early days. I started as an actor, loving the thrill of the stage. But I discovered my creativity was more fully expressed as a producer and writer. Today I still chase the spotlight, but on different stages: speaking engagements, TV interviews, magazine features, and newspapers. These stages feel authentic to who I am now, and they give me the chance to share my passion and purpose—the arts.

I'll be honest: Visibility comes with challenges. Fear, imposter syndrome, and fatigue all play a role. Seeing your own face everywhere can make you wonder if you're oversaturating your audience. But here's the truth: No one sees you as often as *you* see you. Repetition isn't a weakness; it's a part of visibility. Repeat yourself until they—and you—believe you're an authority.

Stepping Outside the Comfort Zone

Fear is the killer of visibility. My advice? Start now. Right now. Stop getting ready to be ready. Start before you're ready.

To prove this to myself, I once committed to a thirty-day Facebook Live challenge. Day one was awkward. I rambled. I felt uncomfortable. Day two was a little better. By day thirty, I had evolved. I was more confident, my messaging was clearer, and I had grown tremendously.

The lesson? Even if you never do the challenge again, the growth stays with you.

Visibility is about creating connection, and connection starts with your story. It's not about you — it's about how your story connects to them. When you speak to their needs and experiences, that's when they listen.

My First Taste of Visibility

My visibility journey started in second grade. I had dyslexia, moved constantly from city to city, and struggled in school. All I wanted was to play Betsy Ross in the school play. Teachers and even my parents told me I couldn't do it. I couldn't read.

But when someone tells me I can't do something, my response is always: "Watch me."

I worked hard to learn and memorize those lines. Not only did I get the role, but I proved to myself that determination creates results. That was my first real taste of visibility.

I wasn't "the girl who couldn't read" anymore. I was Betsy Ross. I was *the girl who could . . . and did.*

That small victory showed me the power of stepping out of my comfort zone and redefining how others saw me. From that moment, the arts became my foundation for visibility. They gave me confidence, stage presence, and connection. They also gave me tools I still use today in business: networking, teamwork, leadership, and yes—marketing.

Creating Visibility for Others

In 2003, my husband Scott and I launched JDS Video & Media Productions to spotlight businesses and help them be seen and heard. Later, we founded JDS Actors Studio, helping students step into the spotlight. Over the years, we've launched more than one hundred careers in acting, directing, producing, and writing. Our bestselling book, *Show Business: Breaking into the Industry as an Actor,* is based on our "Industry Visibility Method."

In 2014, we co-founded JDS Creative Academy, a nonprofit designed to expand our mission even further. JDSCA produces TV shows, live theater, events, and training programs that build confidence and teach career pathways in the arts.

We also created ***DigiFest®***, an international digital media festival, which since 2017 has showcased content creators worldwide. Our TV show *Spirit of Innovation: Arts Across America* is broadcast on ABC and streamed globally, highlighting stories that show the power of the arts to transform lives.

Live theater gives youth and adults the opportunity to step into visibility. I've seen people completely transform—building teamwork skills, collaboration, and the courage to be seen. Watching these transformations is one of my greatest joys.

Beyond organizations, I mentor creatives, coaches, and business leaders to find their visibility through passion and purpose. Sometimes that means guiding a developmentally disabled adult to proudly share their artistic work. Other times, it's helping a professional rebrand themselves so they're known for their true expertise, not just what they've always done.

One client illustrates this well. He was a successful real estate agent but wanted to transition into acting. The challenge? His audience only saw him as "the realtor." His breakthrough came when he consistently showed up as an actor online and in person. Soon he was booking roles, and surprisingly, his real estate business grew, too. Why? Because sharing his authentic story built deeper trust. Visibility opened doors in *both* industries.

Visibility also teaches resilience. Early on, I pitched countless stories and got silence in return. Then silence turned into "no." Eventually, "no" became "not right now." That shift mattered. It meant I was on their radar. With persistence, those "not right now" responses turned into yeses.

Visibility is not about celebrity. It's about connection. It's about showing up so the right people can find you, and your message lands with the right audience.

Visibility Creates Legacy

Steve Jobs once said, *"You can't connect the dots looking forward; you can only connect them looking backward . . . so you have to trust that the dots will somehow connect in your future."*

My dots connect through the arts. They've shaped my passion, my businesses, and my mission. My goal is to show the world how the arts impact life and business, and to move the Arts Across America.

To do that, I must be visible.

If people remember anything about me, I don't want it to be just my name. I want them to remember the impact of the arts: how they change lives, build community, and create growth—both economic and personal.

The arts teach grit, determination, and courage. They teach us to keep showing up even after a "no." They teach us that visibility is worth pursuing because it creates opportunity and allows us to serve the people we're meant to serve.

In the end, there is no impact without visibility.

Diane Strand is an award-winning producer, majority owner of JDS Studios, and founder of nonprofit JDS Creative Academy. A bestselling author and workforce development leader, she creates career pathways in video, performing, and digital arts, launching industry careers. She produces and hosts award-winning programming that breaks barriers and has a mission to move the Arts Across America.

jds-productions.com

THE PROFIT OF PRESENCE: VISIBILITY IS THE FRUIT OF HEALING

CANDACE STUART-FINDLAY

I grew up in a home filled with domestic violence—emotional chaos and physical unpredictability that shaped the very fabric of my childhood. I learned early on how to disappear, how to be small, how to be invisible in order to survive. What I didn't know was that I was encoding those survival strategies into the foundation of my adult life, especially when it came to stepping into visibility.

It wasn't that I didn't want to succeed. I did. I had dreams, vision, and the drive to serve and share. But something inside would pull back when it came time to truly be seen. I would self-sabotage in subtle ways—delay a project, shrink my voice, doubt my worth—because some part of me still believed that visibility equaled danger. That part of me was a child trying to stay safe.

As I've come to understand more deeply over the years, trauma isn't just something that happens and ends. It's something that installs unconscious programs—beliefs, fears, somatic reactions—that run beneath the surface of our conscious lives. These programs don't ask permission. They simply operate, until we become aware enough to pause, question, and choose differently.

Gratitude became the first doorway back to myself. Not the kind of gratitude that denies pain, but the kind that creates enough spaciousness to allow healing to begin. It anchored me into presence. And presence, I found, was the greatest profit of all.

In presence, I could finally meet the parts of me that had been left behind. I began to reclaim them through breath work, meditation, somatic release, and deep inner inquiry. As my nervous system learned to settle, I could begin to expand. I could begin to show up. I could begin to be seen.

And that's when things began to change—not just energetically, but tangibly. Visibility didn't come from a marketing plan or a social media strategy. It came from embodiment. It came from the quiet, rooted confidence of being present in my own skin. People could feel it. Opportunities flowed. My message landed more clearly. And I was no longer afraid to be known.

This is what I've come to know: Visibility is not the goal. Visibility is the fruit of healing. When we clear the distortions of trauma and return to the truth of who we are, we become luminous. Not performative. Not perfect. Just powerfully real.

If you're someone who struggles with being seen, with taking up space, with stepping into your full brilliance—I see you. I've been you. And I promise, you don't have to stay hidden. There is another way.

Start with presence.

Let gratitude soften the edges, which it does ... so effectively. I recommend having a gratefulness practice. The key transformative factor in practicing gratitude is to *feel* it in your body. When I realized the importance of feeling the calming flow of gratefulness and began to practice feeling it, my life dramatically evolved. I was at last able to fully receive blessings of goodness in all manner. I was finally able to heal and release attachment to the trauma of my childhood. That allowed me to identify with who I am today, not loop in a destructive pattern through who I was seventy years ago. That shift alone propelled me forward, creating a comfortability with *being* visible. It finally felt safe to be seen and recognized as a societal contributor. I was then able to move forward without unconsciously creating self-sabotaging mishaps.

Let breath carry you home. I also highly recommend engaging in using breath work to regulate your clarity and purposeful vision. I suggest utilizing a Nasal Abdominal Inhale/Mouth Exhale Box Breathing technique. The Box Breathing technique is used by service members, such as the Navy Seals, to successfully accomplish missions in extremely high-level stress environments.

Box Breathing works like this:

1. Breath in through the nose for a count of four.
2. Hold your breath for a count of four.
3. Exhale through your mouth for a count of six (Or can be four, however having a longer exhale than inhale insures your vagus nerve will activate the release of Acetyl Choline to slow your heartbeat.) (Add a humming or toning sound as you exhale will increase by 15 times the release of nitric oxide into your system.)
4. Pause after the exhale for a count of four.

By engaging in three breaths in this way, you are able to completely reset the type of hormones and neurotransmitters coursing through your body—from adrenaline, noradrenaline, and cortisol to dopamine, serotonin, oxytocin, acetylcholine, and endorphins. It's important to remember that while in the stress reactive sympathetic mode, the prefrontal cortex—which plays a crucial role in executive functions such as decision-making, problem-solving, planning, impulse control, and emotional regulation—is completely bypassed. This region is essential for complex cognitive behaviors and moderating social interactions and is not available while in the stress mode. Breath work will quickly and easily shift you back into the restorative parasympathetic mode, providing access to the prefrontal cortex functionality.

Attempting to make good decisions while stressed is truly point-less. Instead, take a moment to pause and complete three to four box breathing cycles, then reflect internally on what the most appropriate next step may be. You'll then receive clarity and a clear vision of how to successfully move forward.

Let healing make you whole. And as you do, visibility will come—not as a performance, but as a celebration. Not as something to chase, but as something to allow.

The profit of presence is this: When you become fully you, the world finally knows how to find you.

Candace Stuart-Findlay is a meta-physicist, transformational speaker, and author of *Spiritual Transformation Simplified*™ and *The Inter-dimensional Mechanics of Consciousness*. Founder of the Empowered Whole Being Foundation and Press, she blends quantum biology, metaphysics, and spiritual insight to guide Intuitive Empaths worldwide. Her work supports others in awakening to their true self, releasing limitation, and living with clarity, purpose, and joy.

empoweredwholebeing.com

VISIBILITY—THE MISSING LINK TO A PAIN-FREE WORLD

DR. THAY JOE TAN

I *dedicate this chapter with deepest gratitude to my ex-wife Claudia who supported me in every aspect most of our twenty-five mutual years. Without her, my success would not have been possible.*

First of all, congratulations for holding this book in your hands—this chapter might change your life . . . forever.

The Challenge— A World of Pain

Hundreds of millions of people all over the world suffer from pain—e.g., 80 million in the United States, 28 million in the United Kingdom, and 23 million in Germany. This equals about a quarter of the population, so there is a one in four chance that YOU might be one of them.

Because pain is so debilitating, people cannot move, walk, work, even sleep—and they certainly cannot enjoy an active life. Not only is the patient in pain suffering and compromised, but their surroundings are too:

- Their next of kin have to assist them, which costs time and energy (physical and mental).

- Co-workers have to compensate for their underperformance or absence by working more.
- Employers have to either find and pay for a temporary substitute or shoulder increased workloads.

The dilemma of being in pain is not limited to personal suffering, discomfort, and being a burden to their family, friends, and coworkers. It also has a negative financial impact:

- expenses for medication, doctors' visits, hospital stays, operations, rehabilitation, sick leave
- lack of contributions to social security and reduced pension

This interconnected web of impact highlights how pain not only affects individuals but also reverberates throughout families, workplaces, and the broader community and social economy.

The Solution—The Revolution

The primary reason millions of people suffer from pain is that they and their practitioners (doctors, naturopaths, acupuncturists, chiropractors, osteopaths or other eligible therapist) are unaware that there is a proven methodology that can eliminate pain instantly.

It can take as little as ONE tiny acupuncture needle for the patient and as short as ONE weekend for the practitioner to get trained in the groundbreaking methodology of *Turbo*Acupuncture® for instant pain elimination.

Doc PainFree™—The Man Who Moves the Needle

If you're wondering who I am to make this bold statement: I'm Dr. Thay Joe Tan, a multiple international award-winning acupuncture physician, speaker, trainer, and bestselling author of *Instant Pain Elimination*. I am also the originator of *Turbo*Acupuncture® for Instant Pain Elimination and the founding director of one of Europe's largest physician-led practices for acupuncture located in Stuttgart, Germany.

I literally move the needle between my fingers when I eliminate some-one's pain, but also in the sense of freeing the world from pain.

The Visibility Booster

The jaw-dropping results of inserting a tiny little needle just very shallow in the right spot were so mind blowing and literally almost too good to be true that I started to ask patients for testimonials. A lady with longstanding pain that couldn't be helped by various pain killers, including opioids, said that with one needle I took the pain out of her shoulder, and with another needle her back pain was gone. A patient with neck pain said he felt twenty years younger.

My work has been featured on ABC, NBC, Fox, CBS and rec-ognized in *The Wall Street Journal,* which increased the visibility of *Turbo*Acupuncture® even more. Subsequently I have been inter-viewed by Jack Canfield and had the opportunity to share the stage with Apple co-founder Steve Wozniak, Dr. Phil, Charley Sheen, Michael Douglas and Catherine Zeta-Jones, and Mel Gibson. The pinnacle of my visibility was when I had the honor of introduc-ing *Turbo*Acupuncture® for Instant Pain Elimination at the United Nations Headquarters in New York as THE new revolutionary gold standard in pain therapy and the global solution to pain.

Simplify Complexity—The Five Keys to Instant Pain Elimination

No matter what kind of (physical) pain you might have, eliminating pain really comes down just to five keys:

Key #1: Having an open mind

Key #2: Understanding pain

Key #3: Having the right methodology

Key #4: Having the right system

Key #5: Having the right practitioner (if you are the patient) or teacher (if you are the practitioner)

I have elaborated on the first two keys in my previous Amazon bestselling book *The One Big Thing*, which I had the privilege to co-author with Brian Tracy and other experts from around the world.

In this chapter I will focus solely on the three remaining keys.

Key #3: The Right Methodology—TurboAcupuncture®

Among all existing therapeutic modalities I've encountered, *Turbo*Acupuncture® is by far the quickest and most reliable way to eliminate pain; I haven't seen anything that comes close to it. Even though it might be not the right one therapy for everybody, in my personal experience, it helps nineteen out of twenty patients get rid of their pain. I think a 95 percent success rate is unheard of in any other method.

Key #4: The T.A.N. System™—The Practitioner's GPS to Eliminate Pain

T.A.N. is the acronym for the *Turbo*Acupuncture® Navigation system. To make it easy for practitioners to find THE ONE point among theoretically 28 million points and about four hundred classical Chinese acupuncture points, I developed the T.A.N. System™ worksheet, which outlines the algorithm and shows how to identify and exactly locate THE one point that is most likely to eliminate the pain (more or less) instantly.

Key #5: The Certified TurboAcupuncturist™—The Owner of the Power Over Pain

If you are in pain, a certified *Turbo*Acupuncturist™ in your area can help you get rid of pain with a 90 to 95 percent probability. It will feel like magic as your longstanding pain vanishes within seconds or minutes. Once gone, it will usually come back after a day or so, but not as severe as it was before. That's why you need a few treatments until it is gone for good.

If you are a practitioner and want to act in your full therapeutic capacity by owning the power over pain, then the *Turbo*Acupuncture® Certification Master Program is what you need. In one transformational weekend, you will discover the essential fundamentals of Chinese medicine plus the secret behind *Turbo*Acupuncture® for Instant Pain Elimination, including hands-on training. This will empower you to finally release your patients from their years and often decades of suffering. Your unique skill of instant pain elimination will help you magnetically attract and fill your practice with new premium-paying patients, thus generating a new stream of revenue for you.

My Gift Is Your Gift—Your Golden Ticket to Become Pain-Free

I believe that I was gifted by God (nonbelievers may better relate to the Universe) with two superpowers:

> **My superpower #1:** Eliminate pain with just ONE needle.
>
> **My superpower #2:** Train other practitioners with zero previous knowledge in just ONE weekend how to dominate pain. I literally hand over to them the power over pain.

I further believe that I'm supposed to forward this gift to those who will value it as a Golden Ticket:

1. patients who are happily willing to pay the practitioner's fee for eliminating their pain and being released from their sufferings
2. practitioners who are craving to own the power over pain and catapult their therapeutic competency into a totally new dimension, and who understand that the investment for the training and certification is financed by their (new) patients

Dr. Tan's Pain-Free REALITY World Tour™—The Fast Track to Get Rid of Your Pain at Your Doorstep

In December 2022 I decided to declare my frequent travels as Dr. Tan's Pain-Free REALITY World Tour to give patients in pain the unique opportunity to meet me and become pain-free.

Dr. Tan's Pain Free REALITY World Tour™ started in January 2023 in Singapore, visited London and other cities in the UK more than twenty times, went three times to the Philippines and to Cameroon, Indonesia, Romania, The Netherlands, Sri Lanka, the United States and several cities in Germany.

Example #1: In the Philippines, twenty-nine pain patients in Buscalan, a remote mountain village twelve hours north of Manila, became pain-free or almost pain-free. Two of them were even bedridden and could walk again.

Example #2: In Cameroon, two of my *Turbo*Acupuncture® MASTER students co-hosted my annual global summit on *Turbo*Acupuncture® for Instant Pain Elimination. Over three days, we treated eighty patients. One didn't respond at all. Two were 50 percent better, one was 25 percent better, and the remaining seventy-six patients became pain-free or almost pain-free on the spot.

Your Next Best Step

If you want Dr. Tan's Pain Free REALITY World Tour to come to your city so you can claim your birthright to become pain-free, feel free to contact me.

Legal disclaimer: The aforementioned reflects the author's personal experience. No promise of healing or feeling better is given.

Dr. Thay Joe Tan, MD PhD DMD/DDS (aka Doc PainFree™) is a physician, dentist, and multiple international award-winning acupuncture expert, speaker, trainer and bestselling author on Instant Pain Elimination. He is the originator of *Turbo*Acupuncture® for Instant Pain Elimination and the founding director of one of Europe's largest physician-led practices for acupuncture located in Stuttgart, Germany.

www.linkedin.com/in/thepainfreerealityworldtour/?locale=en_US

FROM FEAR OF THE STAGE TO SPEAKING AROUND THE WORLD

TYLER WATSON

A stage. Something I once vowed I would never step onto. Speaking in front of people. Something I promised myself I would never do again.

Fast-forward, and I have been on some of the biggest stages in the world, speaking to audiences of more than five thousand as well as some of the most intimate gatherings with just a handful of people.

I went from a starving massage therapist making fifteen dollars a session to creating millions of dollars in revenue and impacting hundreds of thousands of lives. And I did it while keeping my sanity, having plenty of free time, and spending evenings with my kids at ballet, soccer, and gymnastics.

I'm Tyler Watson, an Elite Performance Coach and creator of the Cellular Alignment Technique, a process to help people make lasting changes in minutes instead of years, and I want to share my journey with you. Whether you are just starting out or have been coaching for years, if you want to get on stages, make money doing it, and still maintain a thriving balanced lifestyle, this is for you.

If you love to struggle, refuse to take responsibility, or are here just for information, skip this chapter. My goal is to push you, challenge you, and get you to step into the version of yourself you know you are capable of becoming.

A Quick Backstory

I have always wanted to help people. But growing up, my examples were not ideal. It was not my parents' fault, and I am grateful for all they went through, but watching my mom go through more than six divorces and my dad go through three left me with deep questions about my own value.

When they first separated, I was twelve. I felt it was all my fault. That belief pulled me into depression for six years, wrapped in addictions to pornography and video games and haunted by suicidal thoughts. I would lie in bed wondering if anyone would even care if I was gone, then wake up the next day, put on a smile, get straight As, and earn titles like MVP and class president, all to fill an internal void.

I was terrified of relationships; I was certain I would fail. And public speaking? Forget it. When I was in school, after being laughed at and mocked for my teeth, I swore I would never speak in front of a group again.

But deep down, I knew there had to be something bigger.

That something bigger came when I met the woman who is now my wife. She's my partner, my confidant, and the one who helped me see the power of what I now teach: the ability to change quickly, step into your power, and create success regardless of your past.

Discovering Alignment

Through learning about mindset, and more importantly, physiology, I went from a fearful, doubting, self-sabotaging man to speaking on global stages alongside Les Brown, Ted McGrath, Russell Brunson, Sharon Lechter, John C. Maxwell, Ray Higdon and countless other incredible leaders. During my first year as a coach, after struggling for months, it finally all started to click, and I made more than six figures in seven months.

One of the principles that changed everything for me was realizing that everything has a pattern, a vibration. Fear, anxiety, self-sabotage—these are just patterns stored in the body. They can become addictions. Just like you can be addicted to sugar, you can be addicted to struggle, rejection, or falling short.

And just as you can have allergies to certain foods, you can be allergic to success, whether that is making $10,000 or $100,000 a month, keeping more than you spend, or allowing yourself to feel joy.

If you do not have what you truly want, it's because some part of you, at a cellular level, is addicted to the struggle and allergic to success.

This is where identity comes in. Your identity is not just in your mind; it's in every cell of your body. Cells have memory, just as muscles do. When you shift that cellular memory into what I call alignment, the addictions and allergies dissolve. You enter a state of choice.

Speaking Without Sabotage

If you want to be visible, whether on stage, in your business, or in your life, you must create an identity that can handle success without burning out, sabotaging, or breaking down.

The test is simple: Set a big goal. Not for the goal itself, but for the pressure it creates. The triggers that come up are your opportunity to shift in real time.

I have seen clients go from years of struggle to breakthroughs in weeks.

- Doug hit consistent six-figure months.
- Kiana turned her business and marriage around from the brink of divorce.
- Taren went from zero to six figures by aligning with his ideal identity.
- Jennie nailed 20k and 30k months consistently after years of never being able to hit even 10k.

The reason most people do not sustain success is they try to force change with repetition, hype, or willpower. That creates temporary wins, but eventually the old identity pulls them back.

If you want real, lasting success, you must become the person capable of receiving and holding it.

The Change Game

I wasn't always good at change. In fact, I resisted it. I wanted stability, no surprises. But God had different plans. I realized that if I stopped changing for the better, I was digressing.

Today, I see change as a game. Every trigger, every form of opposition is a chance to grow. Fight it, and you will struggle. Transform it, and you will accelerate.

One of my favorite examples is Moses leading the Israelites out of Egypt. The journey to the Promised Land could have taken thirteen days, but it took forty years. Why? They left the place of slavery, but not the identity of slaves. Many even wanted to go back.

Physical change without identity change is temporary. Many people spend decades circling the same patterns. The difference between the forty-year route and the thirteen-day route is your speed in confronting and transforming resistance.

Your Stage Awaits

Whether your stage is a literal platform or the stage of your life, the principle is the same. You can wander for decades, or you can choose the short path. Both require growth, but one requires you to face resistance and shift it in the moment.

Being seen will magnify everything inside you, both the strengths and the unhealed patterns. The faster you learn to align, the faster you can handle the spotlight without it burning you.

I encourage you to study these concepts. Learn about the power of your body and how quickly you truly can change.

I believe every person reading this has a message worth sharing. I also believe that the size of your audience will always match the size of the identity you've built to carry it. If you want to expand your impact, you must first expand who you are.

So here is my challenge. Learn this. Study it. Practice it. Don't just collect information and wait for the perfect opportunity. Start now. The sooner you align your identity with the life you want, the sooner that life becomes your reality.

Your audience is already out there. They are waiting for your voice, your story, your unique way of seeing the world. The only question is, will you become the person capable of stepping onto that stage and owning it?

Because once you do, everything changes!

Tyler Watson is an elite performance coach, creator of the Cellular Alignment Technique, and a sought-after international speaker. He helps hundreds of thousands worldwide break through their deepest limitations. Tyler guides entrepreneurs, coaches, and high achievers to align their identity with their vision so they can succeed without burnout and live with purpose, freedom, and impact.

VISIBILITY THROUGH THE REROUTE

KARI WEBER YOUNG

D*ear Reader, if you've picked up this book, there's a good chance you're searching for something—maybe clarity, maybe healing, maybe just the reminder that you're not alone. I want you to know right from the beginning: You are not broken beyond repair. You are human, and humans were never meant to do life—or love—perfectly.*

This chapter is not written from a place of having it all figured out. It's written from the middle of the mess, from the cracks, from the spaces where I once felt invisible in my own marriage. My hope in sharing my journey is not to impress you, but to connect with you—to hold up a lantern so you can see that rerouting is possible, even when the road feels lost.

If my story speaks to you, it's because pain and love are universal. And if there's one truth I've learned, it's this: the same places that hurt us the most can become the very places that heal us.

Every weekend, couples gather at my ranch to celebrate love. They walk hand in hand under the twinkling lights, families wipe tears during vows, and laughter echoes across thirty acres of joy. From the outside, I am surrounded by beauty, love, and everything that should make me feel fulfilled.

But behind the scenes, the reality was that my own marriage was quietly breaking. My husband worked in the oil fields, gone for long stretches of time, while I poured my heart into creating dream weddings for everyone else. I was busy, visible, and successful in the eyes of others—yet invisible in the place that mattered most: my own home.

It's a strange kind of ache, to be the one who creates spaces for love yet feel love slipping from your own life. The joy wasn't there anymore. And in the middle of that loneliness, I did the only thing I knew to do—I prayed. I asked God to show me if I was on the right course, or if everything I had built was just an illusion of success.

Three days later, my entire world rerouted in the most unexpected way.

The Struggle

My husband's oilfield work demanded weeks away from home. He was out there working long hours, while I was here at the ranch, carrying the weight of the dream we had built. On paper, it looked ideal: thirty acres of beauty, a thriving wedding venue, a bed-and-breakfast, a place where love stories blossomed every weekend.

But when the music faded and the last guest left, I often sat alone in the stillness. Surrounded by evidence of other people's happiness, I couldn't escape the emptiness in my own. There is a unique kind of loneliness that happens in marriage when you live in two different worlds—one of distance, one of constant giving.

I was pouring everything I had into making other couples' big days magical, but inside, my own joy was draining. Quietly, I began to wonder: Is this what marriage is supposed to feel like? I didn't want survival. I wanted connection. I wanted the kind of love that made me feel seen.

And that was the painful truth—I was visible to the world, but invisible in my marriage.

That ache pushed me to a crossroads. I could keep pretending everything was fine, or I could face the truth: We were disconnected, and I was breaking under the weight of it.

The Prayer and the Accident

One night, the heaviness became too much. I whispered a prayer that poured straight from my soul:

"God, if I'm on the right course, show me. And if I'm not, reroute me to where You want me to be."

It was the most vulnerable prayer I'd ever spoken. I didn't ask for more success, more weddings, or even for my marriage to instantly heal. I simply asked for clarity.

Three days later, I was in a life-threatening car accident. In an instant, everything I had been holding together shattered. The ranch, the weddings, the busyness—all of it faded as I lay there fighting to breathe.

But that moment wasn't just devastation. It was divine intervention. It was God's way of answering my prayer—not in the way I expected, but in the way I needed.

The accident forced me to see what I had been blind to: I was living visible on the outside but invisible on the inside. I was showing up for everyone but myself. I was creating love stories for others while neglecting my own.

That wreck didn't just stop me. It rerouted me.

And it became the beginning of an awakening.

The Awakening

When life strips you bare, you see things differently. In the quiet of recovery, without the distractions of work and busyness, I was forced to face myself.

I realized I had been measuring visibility by the wrong standards. I thought it was about being admired, noticed, and busy. But real visibility begins with the courage to be honest about who we are and where we truly stand.

I had to admit the cracks in my marriage. I had to name the loneliness that lived in my home. I had to stop pretending that giving to everyone else could fill the void of not giving to myself and to my husband.

And here's the truth I discovered: We are all broken. But broken doesn't mean unworthy. Broken means human. Broken means the light can finally shine through the cracks.

My accident didn't destroy me—it revealed me. It pulled away the masks and gave me a chance to rebuild from the inside out.

I began to see my marriage differently. Instead of resenting the distance and strain, I started asking: How can we use this reroute to build something stronger? How can we honor the cracks instead of hiding them?

I learned that visibility in marriage looks just like visibility in life. It means showing up with honesty. It means saying, "This is where I am. This is what I need. This is how I feel." It means being brave enough to see and be seen, even in the hard moments.

That was my awakening: Visibility is not perfection—it's presence.

The Couples Reroute Method

From my own journey, I created what I now call the Couples Reroute Method—a way for couples to find their way back to each other when life has pulled them apart.

It's built on four steps:

1. Awareness—You can't change what you won't acknowledge. Name the cracks. Be honest about where you are, even when it hurts.
2. Communication—Visibility begins with vulnerability. Share your truth without blame, and listen to your partner's truth with compassion.
3. Realignment—Ask together: What do we want our marriage to look like? Create a shared vision, set new boundaries, and make small changes to honor your connection.
4. Connection—Rebuild intimacy through small, consistent actions. A walk. A prayer. A moment of laughter. Choosing each other, again and again, until love feels alive.

Rerouting doesn't mean your marriage is broken beyond repair. It means you are willing to adjust the map and travel together in a new direction.

Visibility isn't about being seen in the spotlight. It's about being willing to be seen in your truth. For me, that truth came through distance, struggle, and a near-death reroute. It taught me that the greatest visibility begins not on a stage, but in the sacred space of our closest relationships.

Your marriage doesn't need to be perfect. It needs to be present. It needs two people willing to face the cracks, reroute when needed, and choose each other again and again.

This is my mission. This is my work. And this is just the beginning.

The full story—the lessons, the healing, and the path to visibility in love—will be shared in my upcoming book, releasing December 2026. My prayer is that it becomes a gift to couples everywhere who are ready to reroute and begin again.

Kari Weber Young discovered her gift for inspiring others at age eighteen when she was crowned Mason County Forest Festival Queen and gave her first keynote. Since then, she has spoken internationally, sharing stages with Les Brown and other great mentors. She now leads as the Couples Reroute Coach, transforming marriages worldwide.

kariweberyoung.com

EMBRACING YOUR UNIQUE
YOU IN AN AGE OF AI

KIMBERLY WEITKAMP

A I is the newest, prettiest, coolest, funnest buzzword when it comes to marketing. Everyone thinks it's the best thing since sliced bread. It's so simple to sit down in front of your favorite AI tool and ask: "Write me an email. Write me a social post. Write me something for my business and for myself."

But here's the reality: you want to partner with the AI. You don't want it to completely subsume your voice—in your marketing, your messaging, and in your online presence.

Being visible in an age dominated by AI is, now more than ever, related to showing up as your unique you.

For those who are just starting out, it's tempting to think we can completely create our entire marketing strategy, brand voice—everything we could ever want—strictly with the use of AI. But this is a huge missed opportunity for you to show up as you.

Here's the deal: AI is a big learning model. What does that mean? It means it reads everything it can find online and everything put into it by its users. The more people use it, the more broad and generic it becomes, because it has a larger base to pull from.

So how can you use AI in a way that lets you show up as your unique self?

Use it as a partner. Use it as a sounding board. Use it in a way that lets you regain your time, so that you can show up more *you* than ever before.

Are you quirky? Do you like hiking? Do you like painting redwoods in the middle of the forest? What is it that you like? What are your personal lived experiences?

Those are the types of things you don't necessarily want to add into AI. Instead, keep them for yourself and share those stories as part of the content AI creates for you.

Structure, framework, flow—all of that can be outsourced, at least partially, to AI. The rest? Make sure to add *you*—your story, your lived life.

A Story of Self-Expression

When I was a kid, I had a very unique sense of fashion. Every day, I chose differently colored or patterned clothes (that often clashed). My parents gave me this freedom, and I kept this up for years.

One day, another adult turned to my father, who was dropping me off at school, and said something along the lines of "Did you dress her this morning?"

Now, there were a few things wrong with this statement.

First, it was quite insulting to my dad to assume that he couldn't dress his own child—that only a mom could do that. But I was too young to notice that nuance and just found it a little strange.

Second, it completely ignored me, as a person who had an opinion and wanted to express it, even in elementary school.

My dad said, "No, she dressed herself."

The adult continued, "Why would you let her leave the house like this?"

My dad answered, "It's her version of expressing herself."

Exchanges like this kept happening, and eventually I was encouraged to "tone down" the strange dress choices I was making.

So I chose my own form of rebellion: I kept my mismatched socks. I stopped picking the most glaringly clashing patterns, but I kept up my habit of purposely picking mismatched socks every day for years.

That was a quirky, true, lived experience story, and it's not something an AI can just assume.

However, the *idea* for the story came from AI.

When I asked ChatGPT for a list of ideas for stories I could share that showcased the importance of being your unique self, this was one of the prompts. Two sentences sparked an idea, and then I owned it.

I chose the story to share.

The Human Touch

I know tons of people out there who are using AI-generated podcasts, training AI on their voice in various ways, even those who are looking for the day when you can hand off video creation entirely to AI.

And I personally don't think I'll be going down that path.

Here's why: Your face is yours. It's unique in the world, unless you're a twin. Even then, there are subtle differences.

We as humans connect with faces. We remember faces before names. We remember stories before facts. We are hardwired to create real, true connection.

And in an age where connection becomes more nebulous, and where the UN has declared an actual epidemic of loneliness around the world, I think it's more important than ever that when you show up for people in your marketing efforts, you show up as YOU.

If you hand it off to a machine, it begins a degradation of trust. Already, I hear from lots of people who are annoyed at content they see in the world because they know AI wrote it. We can't always identify why we know it was AI, but we can look at something and determine: "That doesn't have a human touch."

There's a difference between AI-powered and partnering with AI to create your content versus wholesale outsourcing to AI and never making human tweaks.

Drawing the Line

So in an age of AI, how can you stand out?

First, decide for yourself: Where is the line you don't want to cross? What will let you keep your uniqueness without "selling out"?

Decide now, before the technology continues to evolve.

I've already seen software that can take ten seconds of video of a person delivering a talk live in a room full of people and turn it into a full-length video that looks real—like that person is delivering in front of a huge stage.

So decide: Is that what you want to do, or is that a line you want to keep for yourself?

I predict that in the next five years, human connection is going to become more important than ever. People will seek out experiences, interactions, and businesses they know are manned by real people.

Personal Items in Marketing

Start choosing your personal items—three things you're happy to talk about with a stranger that have nothing to do with your business.

If you're a health and wellness coach, talking about your daily yoga practice doesn't really count. If you're an accountant, talking about your daily yoga practice absolutely counts. It's all about context.

Choose three things that make you a real, live human being outside the scope of what you deliver. When you do that, people make connections—sometimes on similarities, sometimes on differences.

For example, one person I followed and became a client of for years liked to brew his own beer. Now, I care nothing about brewing beer. But his passion came through when he shared stories about his brewing adventures or visiting breweries when he traveled. I found it entertaining, interesting, and it expanded beyond the business he ran.

So—what are your three personal things?

Being Yourself

Choose to be you.

When you sit down to record a video, don't try to fill somebody else's expectation of what it looks like. Be yourself.

When you're in a room full of people, don't hide who you are.

One of my first lessons in business happened at my very first conference—a copywriting conference. I had been communicating beforehand with a few people who were present at the job fair connected with this conference. One person I met hired me on the spot and then did me the biggest favor ever: She told me why she almost didn't hire me.

She said: "You know, based on your email communication, I didn't think you'd be a fit for this company. You were too stiff, too formal. But after meeting you, I can see you have such great energy—it fills the room—and you're the exact right fit."

That was the best advice I could have received early in my career. I had been trying to be somebody I wasn't.

I didn't have twenty years of corporate experience like most of the other people in the room. I didn't have ten years of work experience like 95 percent of them. What I had was *me*—my youthfulness, my love of travel, my adventure-seeking ways.

That's what drew people to me. It's what made me stand out. And it's what made people say: "This is the person I want to hire."

When you hide who you are and hide your lived experience, you discount yourself. You prevent others from finding the true support they're looking for.

In conclusion, in an age when AI is only going to grow more powerful, it's more important than ever for you to show up as you.

Show up as your unique, authentic self. Decide now where your personal line is—where AI helps, and where AI damages your visibility.

Kimberly Weitkamp is known as the Audience Converter. With more than ten years of experience, she works with coaches and online entrepreneurs to craft marketing that makes money and aligns with their values, goals, and calendar. She's host of the Top 3 Percent Globally Ranked *More Conversations, Clients & Cash* podcast.

go.theaudienceconverter.com

VISIBLE, VALUABLE, VIABLE—FROM CAREGIVER TO COMMUNITY LEADER

KATE WOODWARD YOUNG AND CARRIE CASEY

March 19, 2020, is burned into our memory. The ER was already humming when my phone started buzzing in my pocket. Monitors chirped, someone called "Room Four," gloves snapped, and under it all was that persistent vibration—call after call ignored until the text came through: "Call me now 911." I ducked into the supply closet, shoulder pressed against a stack of saline boxes, and called.

"I'm at the center to drop off the kids," my partner said, voice tight. "There's a piece of paper on the door. 'Closed by order of the governor.'"

Silence. In that one breath, my mind ran a dozen calculations: patient load, shift change, which coworkers had kids, who could swap, how long grandparents could manage, how fast this virus would move through a city. I could see the preschool's glass door in my mind— blue tape crisscrossing a printed notice, the foyer lights off at 7:02 a.m., and the teacher who always waved through the window ... gone.

We started calling everywhere. Centers. Home providers. A church program. Every voicemail was the same careful script: *For everyone's safety, we're temporarily closed due to COVID-19. We hope to reopen soon.* A neighbor could take the baby until noon if her conference call ended early. An aunt across town could pick up the preschooler after lunch—if her HR looked the other way—if the highways stayed clear—if, if, if. We pieced together a plan for today. Tomorrow? Unknown. Thursday? Don't think that far.

On the way back to the floor, the break-room TV showed the same words scrolling along the bottom: *Closed by order of the governor.* In that moment, it became crystal clear: The economy doesn't run on slogans; it runs on people. And people run on child care. When child care stops, everything slows. When it goes dark everywhere at once, the whole system shudders. That was the day the world noticed child care.

Every field has its own version of that closed door with blue tape on it. It might be the supplier who suddenly stops shipping, the volunteer base that quietly drifts away, or the client pipeline that dries up because no one knows what we do anymore. The details vary, but the pattern is the same: when our work is invisible, people don't think of us until they can't get what we offer—and by then, it's often too late to fix it quickly. Visibility keeps us in the conversation before a crisis hits. And visibility means being ready to make a difference right here, right now—not when it's convenient, not when the stars align, but in the moment our community needs us most.

Visibility isn't vanity—it's the difference between being dismissed as "babysitters" and being recognized as essential infrastructure. It's how we keep our classrooms open, our staff paid, and our mission alive.

Invisibility has a cost. It shows up as empty seats that go unfilled, tuition we feel the need to apologize for, staff we can't retain, and partnerships that never form. We cannot serve if we can't staff and fund our programs. Yet many of us quietly do heroic work behind the scenes while remaining practically invisible to the people who could support us. Our websites still feature stock photos from five years ago—the children in them probably in middle school now. Our faces and voices rarely appear online. Policies are enforced "case by case," teaching families they can negotiate their way out of them. Tours focus on snack menus instead of learning outcomes. The heart is there, but the structure to be seen is missing.

I'll never forget one director—Melissa—who proudly described her program as "the best-kept secret in town." She said it like it was a badge of honor, the way a boutique cupcake shop might talk about a hidden menu. But secrets don't fill classrooms. Her enrollment had been flat for three years. Tours were warm but unfocused. She avoided talking about the value behind tuition. Her Google profile hadn't been updated in months.

A handful of practical changes transformed her results: a one-sentence promise on the home page, a short video introducing herself, a scripted tour that connected features to benefits, weekly updates to her Google profile, a one-page "what to expect" sheet for local employers, and two policies—tuition timelines and late pick-up fees—enforced without apology.

Six months later, her tour show rate had doubled. Enrollment rose about 40 percent over two terms. Teacher retention improved. The biggest surprise? Families expressed gratitude for the clarity, and teachers felt more respected when policies were consistently upheld.

From an employer's perspective:

"Since the center formalized a referral pathway and started sharing staffing stability updates, we've had far fewer last-minute shift call-offs. It's been a game changer for our scheduling."

From a parent's perspective:

"Choosing a program felt easier when the director could explain the learning outcomes clearly and we could see the ongoing training hours for teachers. It gave us confidence we'd found the right place."

That's the power of visibility—it works like a flywheel. It starts with clarity: knowing exactly who we serve and the promise they can count on. Then credibility: proof of expertise, credentials, and outcomes. Consistency follows: the same message everywhere—website, tours, materials. Connection comes next: becoming a hub for employers, libraries, and community partners. Finally, capacity: Visibility funds quality, and quality drives referrals.

Heart alone is not enough. We may care deeply about our work, train our teams, and stretch budgets to keep classrooms open—but a purely service identity can keep us invisible. To step into full leadership, we must embrace the role of CEO of an early learning business. That shift often begins with language: tuition instead of fees, early education instead of daycare, leader instead of babysitter. Boundaries aren't barriers; they're respect in action for teachers, families, and the work itself.

Visibility is not limited to advertising. It's in the everyday micro-habits that signal value: greeting families with a twenty-second explanation of the learning taking place, posting weekly teacher spotlights, wearing name badges, using consistent hallway language about outcomes. It is publishing five key metrics every quarter—teacher tenure, professional development hours, family satisfaction, occupancy rate, and completed safety audits. These are not boasts; they are quiet proof.

Some will still choose to do nothing, saying they're too busy for visibility work. But a semester without it often means empty seats linger, discounts creep in, and hiring becomes harder. The alternative is three months of steady action: thirty days to publish a clear promise, refresh the Google profile with current photos, enforce two key policies, and script the tour. Sixty days to host a parent education night, introduce a new community partner, and start teacher spotlights. Ninety days to refine pricing language, share metrics publicly, and create one formal employer referral pathway. No billboards. No forced TikTok dances—unless, of course, they're in focus and not aimed at the ceiling fan. Just clear, credible, consistent actions that build connection and capacity.

The most important questions we can ask are: Where are we invisible right now—online, in policy, or in partnerships? Which boundary, if enforced, would most increase respect for our team? Do families hear our educational promise before the hours and price? These questions aren't meant to cause guilt—they are meant to spark action. Because visibility isn't just marketing; it's leadership. And leadership means making a difference right here, right now.

This matters more than ever. In every sector, attention has become the new currency. People are busy, distracted, and over-whelmed with choices. When we aren't visible, we're not just over-looked—we're replaced. Someone else is telling a clearer story, showing up with proof, and taking the opportunities that could have been ours. Visibility is not a "someday" project—it's a "today" project. It's the discipline of showing up with clarity, credibility, and consistency so when our community needs help, they already know who to call.

And here's the truth: opportunities rarely knock twice. The moment to stand up, speak out, and be seen doesn't wait for a quieter week on the calendar. It happens in real time, in the messy middle of budgets, staffing, and a to-do list that never ends. We either claim that moment or watch it pass us by. Right here, right now is when trust is built, when partnerships form, and when our value is cemented in the minds of the people who matter most.

There are programs where the staff buzz with energy, classrooms are full, and wait-lists stretch months ahead—not because they're the only option in town, but because the community knows them, trusts them, and talks about them. That doesn't happen by accident. Those leaders decided they would not be a best-kept secret. They decided to be visible, valuable, and viable.

We all face the same choice: Hope the right people stumble across us—or step fully into the role our community needs us to play. We can decide to make a difference right here, right now, by showing up in a way that's impossible to ignore.

We are not babysitters. We are professionals who keep the wheels turning. And the way we do that—right here, right now—is by being visible, valuable, and viable. This is how we protect our teams, fund quality, and serve more families—sustainably.

Kate Woodward Young and Carrie Casey are nationally recognized early childhood experts with more than thirty years each in childcare leadership, training, and business development. Co-hosts of the internationally ranked podcast *Childcare Conversations* and authors of nine books, Kate and Carrie bring practical, real-world solutions that empower leaders, transform schools, and inspire educators to succeed.

kateandcarrie.com